How to Do
BASEBALL
RESEARCH

© 2000 Society for American Baseball Research

Published by The Society for American Baseball Research (SABR)
812 Huron Road, Suite 719, Cleveland, OH 44115
www.sabr.org

Distributed by the University of Nebraska Press
233 North 8th Street
Lincoln, NE 68588-0255
www.nebraskapress.unl.edu

Designed by Glenn LeDoux

Printed and manufactured by EBSCO Media, Birmingham, Alabama

Internet Addresses: To avoid repeating http://, which is the universal starting point
for all Internet addresses, http:// is not shown in this book. Ordinarily, but not always,
the beginning of the Internet address appears as www (for World Wide Web).

How to Do
BASEBALL
RESEARCH

General Editor
Gerald Tomlinson

Chapter Authors
Gerald Tomlinson
Steve Gietschier
Andy McCue
Ted Hathaway
Neal Traven
Cappy Gagnon
Mark Rucker
Tom Shieber
Mark Alvarez
Larry Gerlach

Contributors
A. D. Suehsdorf
Lyle Spatz
Bob McConnell
Dick Clark
Rick Bradley
Leslie Heaphy
Bill Carle
John Husman
Bob Bluthardt
James J. Combs
Clifford Otto
Larry Lester

TABLE OF CONTENTS

INTRODUCTION
by Mark Alvarez

SABR exists because its members love to learn about their game. Some of us are interested in players, some in teams, some in leagues or eras or sections of the country. Some of us chase down the locations of old ballparks. Some of us appreciate the game most through the numbers it generates. Some of us are more interested in personalities and relationships. Some of us tune into baseball's place in our national culture. Some of us are fascinated by equipment and technique. Some of us do our digging by computer. Some of us haven't overcome our suspicion of touch-tone phones. Some of us were fine, even great, players ourselves. Some of us played only in our imaginations. Some of us follow the modern game avidly. Some of us no longer read the daily boxscores.

Every one of us, though—every single member—is part of the great SABR network of friends and colleagues who share not just a love of the game, but a desire to know more about it and a willingness to help to help others do the same.

It's been thirteen years since the Society for American Baseball Research published *The Baseball Research Handbook*. Over that time, there has been, in no small part because of SABR and SABR members, a boom in the study of our game. As SABR's Publications Director, I'm proud that members have made major contributions in correcting the historical record, in shining a brighter light on the Negro Leagues, in demonstrating the useful application of statistics, in asserting and explaining the value of the nineteenth century game, and in fostering the study of baseball as a significant American institution. (By and large, we've all had a lot of fun in the process, too.)

This completely new book is meant as an encouragement and an invitation to anyone, SABR member or not, interested in sampling the joy and satisfaction of digging around a bit in the garden of baseball. The pages that follow are stuffed with the ideas, methods, and suggestions of some of SABR's most experienced researchers. Ten chapters cover the basics of collecting, evaluating, illustrating, and publishing information. Each is written by a different SABR member with special expertise. Editor Jerry Tomlinson has also included a dozen brief but important boxes by yet more SABR specialists, with tips for those interested in particular areas of research, from ballparks to the minor leagues to women in baseball.

This volume, and the information it conveys, is at the core of SABR's purpose. I hope you enjoy it. More important, I hope you enjoy using it.

Chapter One
TEN KEYS TO GOOD RESEARCH
by Gerald Tomlinson

In research, as in most other activities, there are no shortcuts to success, no magic formulas. There are some useful points to keep in mind, however, of which the following ten are fundamental.

1. Break New Ground

The usual reason for doing research is to make an original contribution to knowledge about a particular subject. If a topic has already been thoroughly explored—Joe DiMaggio's 56-game hitting streak in 1941, for example—there is probably no need to research it further. Of course, if you are quite sure you have or can come up with solid evidence for an entirely different truth than the one now accepted, you might decide to go ahead and pursue it. What you don't want to do, though, is merely to repeat, in a different way or in different words, what most well-informed baseball fans already know.

Some new topics are inherently more significant than others. One that is clearly significant is Leo Trachtenberg's "Ken Burns Commits an Error" in the 1996 *Baseball Research Journal*, about film footage in the "Fourth Inning" of Burns's documentary, "Baseball: The American Epic," which aired in 1994. The film implies that the images show Babe Ruth hitting his sixtieth home in 1927. As Trachtenberg explains, the footage must have been shot on a different date. There are no known motion pictures of Ruth hitting his sixtieth homer. Trachtenberg concludes: "By giving us that misleading picture of a celebrated moment in baseball history Burns and his associates have slighted their obligation to historic authenticity." True—and important.

Research into the history of the 1926 Port Huron Saints of the long-defunct Class-B Michigan State League, on the other hand, might not seem very significant. Yet both projects are original, and in their own fields, valuable. Anything that adds to a reader's understanding or knowledge of the game is worthwhile. Recognize, however, that the chances of your research being published are greater (self-publishing excepted) if your topic is of widespread interest.

2. Zero In

A good research topic must be focused. That may sound rather like high-school textbook advice, but it's the simple truth. You can't explore the entire universe of baseball. The topic of "baseball" is broader than the North American continent and as varied as *Aaron to Zuverink*. You have to decide exactly what area of it you intend to research.

Your topic may be broad. It may be narrow. Are you going to produce a comprehensive three-volume history such as David Q. Voigt's *American Baseball*? Or is your goal more modest, something more along the lines of Chris Lamb's "March 17, 1946" in the 1999 *National Pastime*, dealing with Jackie Robinson's first game with the Montreal Royals? Both are focused, but their scope is quite different.

There is no mystery about what focused topics are. They can be found everywhere. Published books on baseball, with rare exceptions, have well-defined coverage. A glance through an issue of *The Baseball Research Journal* or *The National Pastime* will reveal a host of focused topics for brief articles. In fact, you won't see much in print that isn't carefully focused, because zeroing in on a topic—concentrating on a fixed field with distinct boundaries—is almost always essential to publication.

3. Plan Where You're Going

Among writers of fiction, the argument about whether to outline or not to outline has raged for a long time. But among writers of nonfiction, especially book-length nonfiction such as biographies and team histories, there is no such argument. A good outline is a big plus and is often a necessity.

An outline doesn't necessarily have to follow the classic textbook pattern—the rigid alternation of numerals and letters—although some do. Eugene C. Murdock's excellent biography of American League founder Ban Johnson was developed from a full-scale traditional outline. But Ronald A. Mayer's fine *Christy Mathewson: A Game-by-Game Profile of a Legendary Pitcher* has a much simpler organizational plan. As its subtitle suggests, it did not require an elaborate outline. Even when there is meticulous pre-planning, as with Murdock's *Ban Johnson*, the outline is not cast in bronze. Far from it. The outline changes as the work progresses. An outline is a flexible working tool, not a straitjacket.

4. Make Sure the Sources Exist

Graduate students can often tell horror stories about long-term research ruefully abandoned because crucial information couldn't be found. It sometimes happens in baseball research, too, even with experienced researchers at work on major league topics.

The problem is more acute at the minor league level and much more acute with Negro League teams and players. As editors Dick Clark and Larry Lester point out in SABR's *The Negro Leagues Book*, "Despite the publication of career statistics for some prominent Negro Leagues players in recent editions of *The Baseball Encyclopedia*, a complete Negro

Leagues encyclopedia is impossible at present, and won't become possible for years. In fact, many of the statistical lines in 'the record' are dubious and subject to change." The task of statistical research in this field, the editors concede, is mammoth.

The absence of sources, unfortunately, is a danger that is easier to state than to avoid. You may not know that the sources don't exist until you have spent a great deal of time failing to find them. One of the perils of research is that the critical box score may truly be lost forever, the sought-after scrapbook may have gone up in flames.

Yet one of the thrills of research is the uncertainty of the chase, the challenge of pursuit. A truly impossible challenge is seldom enjoyable, however. Abundant sources tend to be more comforting than a lack of sources. Too many dead ends can turn one's thoughts away from research and toward watching reruns of television sitcoms.

5. Find Everything You Can

The word *search* is three fourths of the word *research*, and a researcher's need to search cannot be emphasized too strongly. You want to find out everything you can about your topic. That means digging. At first, especially if you find very little material, you may conclude that not much is available. In some cases, as already noted, you will be right, but more often a thorough search will reveal unexpected sources. You may even find that your topic is a kind of benign Pandora's box. Once you open the box, the sources come flying out.

When I started to research my article "Lefty George: The Durable Duke of York," I expected the sources to be mainly small-city newspaper articles from Lefty's years on the mound. He was a minor league pitcher for most of his career, and he had died more than a quarter of a century before I began my research. I had no inkling that in 1954 a trade association In York, Pennsylvania, had published a booklet about this hardy hurler (*50 Years in Baseball with Lefty George*) and certainly none that his daughter would send me a large carton of clippings, letters, photos, and even a Columbus Red Birds contract from Lefty George's personal collection of memorabilia. One thing led to another, and the microfilm of the old and excellent York *Dispatch* proved to be just one source among many.

6. Ask Other Researchers

"Tell me what you know about my topic," is not always an easy question for one researcher to ask another. The uniqueness of your project, and your desire to be the recognized authority on it, may keep you working in libraries for hours, a dedicated, solitary toiler. But no amount of page-turning and microfiche-scanning can replace the collegial act of posing the right question to the right fellow researcher at the right time.

Of course, it's hardly fair to ask others to do your work for you. If you can find the answer you need in a printed or an on-line source, by all means do so. But if you've hit an unyielding barrier, if you're faced with too many conflicting accounts, or if you can't

"WELL, YOU'LL WANT TO..."

by A. D. Suehsdorf

Most of my stuff has taken shape after many hours with books and microfilm. I'm not suggesting that this is the only way to write an article, but judging by the copy I edit these days, and by the queries I get from time to time, I feel that your primary sources are less important than how you integrate and interpret whatever comes to hand. Going farther afield, exploring all the dusty trails and unpaved byways, often leads to the small surprises and odd facts — "I didn't know that before!"— that add pungency as well as verisimilitude to an article. The suggestions that follow are just that: possibilities to that end. (And if you achieve less than you'd hoped, be prepared to rewrite.)

1. **Give yourself a basic library of first-rate baseball books.** These books offer authoritative perspectives on the game. Refer to them frequently and get to know them well: the Harold Seymour trilogy; *Total Baseball* and/or *The Baseball Encyclopedia*; the David Porter *Biographical Dictionary of American Sports: Baseball*; *The Bill James Historical Baseball Abstract*; anything by Donald Honig, Charles C. Alexander, Eugene Murdock. or Robert W. Creamer; Paul Dickson's *Baseball Dictionary*; Robert Obojski's *Bush League*; Marc Okkonen's *Baseball Uniforms of the 20th Century*; the Cohen-Neft *World Series*; Joe Reichler's *Baseball Trade Register*. SABR's resources such as *Baseball's First Stars*, *The Negro Leagues Book*, and Phil Lowry's *Green Cathedrals* are invaluable. Add anything that elaborates on your own special interests.

2. **Pick your article ideas carefully.** What is really to be learned by the research you are about to undertake? Your topic doesn't have to be earth-shaking, but your enthusiasm for it, whether you are talking personalities or events, should communicate the unique and wonderful flavor of baseball.

3. **Be careful and judicious.** Baseball loves to perpetuate its legends—all five versions of them. See how many ways Brooklyn's "three-men-on-third" story has been told. Or the one about the bird under Casey Stengel's hat. Any repetition of them should be tracked to original sources, if you can. Game dates for such items may take some digging, but they are known, and you should try to get as close to the original source as you can. On the other hand, I found three versions of who "discovered" Walter Johnson and, inasmuch as the trail was too dim to prove any of them, for the fun of it I used all three.

4. Recognize that some problems are insoluble. No matter how careful you've been, difficulties may remain. Is Joe Wood Smokey or Smoky? *Total Baseball*, Harold Seymour, and Roger Angell have it –ey. *The Baseball Encyclopedia*, David Porter, and L. Robert Davids have it –y. Actually, among experts, -ey has a seven to four edge.

5. Do your homework. Know what you want to ask when you're lucky enough to meet with old players. They can be garrulous without being very informative. Or, on the other hand, they can surprise you with some juicy stuff you didn't know about or expect. During the one talk I had with Edd Roush—I had phoned to ask him a fact or a date; something inconsequential—he suddenly launched into a tirade about John McGraw and the contract battles he used to have with him. Marvelous!

6. Backstop your article. You should have a file of source material four times as thick as the pages of your article. Type your notes as soon as possible after an interview. It's a rare writer who doesn't find a few indecipherable scribbles among them. Check duplicate sources. A Yankee-Tiger game story in the New York *Times* may be your principal account, but see what the Detroit *News* had to say about it, too. As you probably know, morning papers are best for detailed game accounts, while the afternoon papers often have feature stories containing quotes and anecdotes.

7. Become acquainted with the style of the publication you are writing for. Which numbers are printed as numerals, which are spelled out? What abbreviations are permitted? Is *ballclub* one word or two? It's *right field* or *right fielder* but *righthanded* or *righthander*. This is the editor's and proofreader's job, but making it easier on them may reduce the blue penciling of your manuscript and the persistence of inadvertent errors.

8. Be patient and be persistent. Research is small carpentry. You have to enjoy the details. So be alert to how they fit together to make the seamless article you intend.

understand why a source seems to be obviously incorrect, you may want to seek the advice of one or more other researchers.

For beginning researchers the decision to seek advice may be easier and more essential than for old pros. If you're a novice researcher, as I was in 1979, you might ask, as I did Clifford Kachline, then the historian at the National Baseball Hall of Fame and Museum in Cooperstown, "Is there any way I can find the major and minor league career stats of James (Ripper or Rip) Collins?" Cliff responded with an order form for *Minor League Baseball Stars*, Volume I, and a SABR membership form. I promptly filled out both.

7. Be Careful

Although getting it right is the essence of research, the task can be daunting. Newspaper typos are common. Factual errors abound in baseball reporting. A harried sportswriter, working under a pressing deadline, makes a careless and, to him, not very consequential mistake. The mistake is then picked up by other writers and later by baseball researchers. Although repeated ad infinitum, the slip-up is just as much an error in the twenty-first century as it was on the day it was made.

The most accomplished writers and researchers can fall into unexpected traps. In a recent *New Yorker* article, Roger Angell, writing about Don Zimmer, identified the old Class-D PONY League as the "Pennsylvania-Ohio-New York League." It sounds right, even fairly obvious, but it isn't. The O in PONY stands not for Ohio but for Ontario. If a great baseball writer like Roger Angell and the fact checkers at *The New Yorker* can go wrong, so can we all.

Richard Altick in his book *The Scholar Adventurers* makes the point that there is no major figure in history—he is talking about writers and other literary figures—"whose biography has been innocent of falsehoods and half-truths, placed there by an early memoirist and then uncritically repeated from writer to writer—and usually embroidered in the transmission—until at last they are disproved by the researcher." The same is true of baseball biographies and histories.

On the other hand, instead of all sources agreeing on an untruth, two sources may disagree on what should be a matter of cold fact. Or three sources may disagree. Or four. The more research you do, the more amazed you will become at the amount of misinformation that has found its way into print. It's your job as a researcher to uncover the truth, to reconcile the conflicting reports, to make your own sound judgment from the best evidence available. It's quite a job.

8. Keep Exact Records

Most researchers have had the experience of losing track of their sources. You probably will face the same dilemma sooner or later. Your notes are perfect, or seem to be, but where in the world did that fascinating bit of information come from? You have the name, date, place, score, or whatever down on paper or on a floppy disk. You're pretty sure the fact you cite is correct. But the source—"There had to be source," you tell yourself—is missing. You need that source.

This does not mean that for a brief article you need to keep a sheaf of note cards. Your research is not intended to earn you an advanced academic degree. Still, you ought to know where each item of information in your manuscript came from. If the editor says, "Prove it," you should be able to do so. Proving it does not necessarily mean producing a bulging note card file. It may mean nothing more than having a photocopy of a box score, a clipping from a newspaper, a page reference to a *Sporting News* article, a recorded quote from an interview—anything that shows you have an actual, verifiable source and not just a guess or a recollection.

9. *Don't Procrastinate*

Somerset Maugham once wrote a short story about a man who spends most of his life assembling notes for what he believes will be a monumental work. The man grows older and older. His notes pile up higher and higher. He dies, never having gotten a word on paper.

To a dedicated researcher, that story may seem to be more like truth than fiction. It's easy, and even defensible, to defer writing until every last detail has been tracked to earth. It's doubly easy if the researcher feels uneasy (or possibly terrified) about the process of writing. For many researchers, finding facts is fun; presenting them clearly on paper is drudgery.

Writing, after all, is work, a special and demanding kind of work, just as playing shortstop is a special and demanding kind of work, and some people can do it better than others. No amount of effort, and surely no handbook of instruction, will turn a nonwriter into a Roger Kahn or a Donald Honig. Researching and writing are two different skills. Not every outstanding researcher is an equally fine writer, although mastery of writing does give the researcher a great advantage. For one thing, it helps to make careful research accessible to a larger public, as witness Charles C. Alexander's superb biographies of Ty Cobb, John McGraw, and Rogers Hornsby.

10. *Plan to Revise*

No one can write a perfect first draft. Anyone who insists that he or she can do so has a tenuous grip on reality, or a tin ear, or an inflated ego, or all three. It's simply impossible. Revision is essential, even for geniuses. Isaac Asimov, one of the most prolific writers of the twentieth century, admitted that he revised every manuscript once. Most good writers revise their material several times. You don't have to emulate Oscar Wilde, who claimed to spend the morning putting in a comma and the afternoon taking it out again. But you should plan to spend quite a bit of time improving your first draft. You'll be surprised at how much better you can make it.

Even so, minor mistakes are probably inevitable. Count on it: If the journal containing your article reaches you on June first, by June second or third you'll have come across something that really should have been in it. Or, on your first reading of the printed version, you'll see a glaring error you overlooked a dozen times in the manuscript. Or an experienced researcher will read your material and give you (too late) valuable suggestions for changes and additions. Don't despair. It happens to everybody. Keep calm, keep researching, and keep writing. Some day if your article goes into an anthology (or your book into a second printing) you'll be able to revise it for future readers. If not, *c'est la vie*. Resolve to try harder next time.

When Casey Stengel said, "You could look it up," he might have been talking directly to SABR members. Casey's famous challenge is a quick definition of research, and research is what many SABR members like to do. It is, in fact, the lifeblood of the organization. Conceiving and completing a first-rate research project is not always easy, but it is almost always worth the effort. Research can be educational, and it can be fun, and anyone can try it. Best of all, when research gets difficult, as it often does, there's lots of help. Research assistance in the Age of Information is widely accessible. You don't have to quit your day job or live within fly-ball distance of a major library. You just have to know where to look it up.

Your Local Library

Next to the ballpark, many SABR members call the library the place they like best. Local libraries come in many shapes and sizes, but they are all worth a visit. People are sometimes intimidated by libraries, but there is no reason for that. Libraries are established and maintained to serve people, to serve you. No one will make that point more strongly than professional librarians themselves. You should make your local library your first stop as a baseball researcher.

But remember, libraries vary. If you live in a large city, your local library is probably part of a library system with a headquarters, neighborhood branches, and substantial resources. The New York Public Library, for example, a private institution with four major research libraries and eighty-five branches throughout Manhattan, the Bronx and Staten Island, is quite imposing. Its book collection, numbering in the millions of volumes, has been called "the diary of the human race." If you live in a smaller city or town, your local library will certainly be more modest, but it still may be a significant institution with holdings and services appropriate to the size of your community.

Resolve to use your local library fully, regardless of its size or budget, and leave no research stone unturned. The staff members there, even if they are not baseball savvy, can get you started. They can show you around the place and introduce you to the sources in their holdings. In addition, thanks to the Internet and the World Wide Web, they can show you how to open doors to other libraries around the world. Some local libraries can be of more help than others, but all of them can provide basic assistance to SABR researchers. When you look it up, start there.

A Word About Archives

Some SABR members may begin their research in a library and then continue their work in an archives. (That's right, "an archives" is correct. The word ends with "s," but it is both singular and plural.) Others might not be exactly sure what the word "archives" means or how an archives differs from a library. So here's a primer. Archives and libraries are cousins, but they are not the same thing. The primary difference is this: Libraries hold materials that, in general, are not unique and are available elsewhere, in other libraries. Archives hold materials that, in general, are unique and are not available elsewhere, at least in their original format. When we speak of library materials, we are talking about books, serials (periodicals), newspapers, and pamphlets. Archival materials, on the other hand, include manuscripts (that is, the papers of individuals or families) and records (that is, the papers of private and public institutions, including government). Obviously, library materials, like the latest edition of *Total Baseball* or the current issue of *The Sporting News*, can be found in many places. But archival materials, such as the papers of Branch Rickey, can be found in only one place. Library materials often circulate. That is, patrons can, by following certain procedures, take them home for a period of time. Archival materials never circulate. Patrons must use them only within the confines of the institution that holds them.

Sometimes an archives stands alone as a separate entity, perhaps with a small reference library included within. Sometimes an archives is contained within a library. This is especially true at colleges and universities whose libraries often contain special collections or manuscripts departments. And sometimes an archives and a library are co-equal parts of a larger organization, such as a state historical society. The important point for SABR members to understand is that both libraries and archives are places where research can be done. Both have reference staffs eager to help. But whereas almost any library can get a novice baseball researcher started, only a few archives, those that hold baseball-related materials, can do the same.

What Reference Is—And What It Isn't

Some small libraries direct patrons walking through the door for the first time to a general information desk or to the circulation desk, but most libraries and archives have a reference desk or a reference department. New researchers should start there. Reference librarians and reference archivists will help you all they can. They are not only trained to do so; they are paid to do so; they want to do so. In fact, the American Library Association and the Society of American Archivists have published guidelines that direct reference personnel to treat patrons courteously and helpfully. If there is one shining exception to the perception of bureaucratic apathy in the United States, it can be found in the reference rooms of America's libraries and archives.

Still, it is important for researchers to know that reference librarians and archivists can do only so much. Information professionals, as these people are sometimes called, often have to draw a line between what they can do and what they cannot do, and sometimes patrons get upset when they don't receive the kind of assistance they have anticipated. So here are some rules to help new researchers deal comfortably with reference staffs:

❶ They cannot do your research for you. Reference personnel are trained to help you find the sources you need to do your own research. They can tell you what items they have in their collection and direct you to them. They can help you understand the card catalog or the online catalog. They can show you how to use microfilm readers. They can assist you in using computers. They can help you contact other libraries and archives. They can suggest research paths that you might not have otherwise considered. But they cannot do line-by-line investigative work for you.

❷ They respond better to specific questions than to vague or open-ended questions. Give reference personnel a fighting chance. Ask a precise question that expresses exactly what you are looking for. If, for example, you are interested in the 1947 World Series game in which Cookie Lavagetto broke up Bill Bevens's no-hitter in the ninth inning, do not begin your inquiry by asking a reference librarian, "Do you have any books on baseball?" Ask instead, "Can you show me how to find books that might discuss the 1947 World Series?" or "Can you show me how to look at newspaper accounts of the 1947 World Series?"

❸ They cannot be expected to offer opinions on baseball matters. Reference personnel do not have to be experts in baseball history or even interested in baseball at all. They are generalists who are trained to help patrons find the information important to them. Thus, if you want to find a list of all the pitchers who have won 300 games, say so. But do not ask, "Who do you think was the best pitcher in the twentieth century?"

❹ They can be trusted not to share your research with others. Some SABR members might be reluctant to speak frankly with information professionals out of fear that some other researcher might learn about or "steal" their ideas.

This hesitancy can lead to rather guarded and awkward research queries that prove to be not very helpful. Fear not. Reference personnel have a code of ethics that specifically forbids them from betraying any confidences. You may talk with them freely and know that the originality of your project will be protected.

❼ They should not be expected to answer trivia questions. Reference personnel are professionals dedicated to assisting serious patrons. They generally work in institutions that are understaffed and underbudgeted. So do them a favor. Don't ask questions that reasonable people would consider trivial. If you want to know what number Stan Musial wore, fine. If you want to know what size shoe he wore, take it elsewhere.

Your Library's Collection

Traditionally, patrons found out what books their library held by using a card catalog. They could search the catalog, looking for books by perusing author cards, title cards and subject cards. Nowadays, many libraries have computerized their catalogs, and patrons must learn new search techniques. A reference librarian can show you how to use the online catalog, sometimes called the OPAC (for Online Public Access Catalog). You can then use the catalog to determine exactly which baseball books your library holds, either in the reference room or in the general collection, often called the "stacks."

The reference staff can also tell you whether the library catalogs its collection using the Dewey Decimal System (which classifies baseball books in the 796.357 section) or the Library of Congress System (which puts baseball in the GV861 - GV881 sections). Once you know this, you can use catalog call numbers to find specific books.

General Reference Books

Once you have checked the baseball sources your library holds, you may be interested in looking more broadly to identify sources that your library does not have. To do this, you should start by becoming familiar with several of the fundamental resources found in almost every reference room. Here are a few of the most useful, many of which now also appear on CD-ROM and online:

1. *Subject Guide to Books in Print*. 1957-present. New York: R.R. Bowker, 1957-present. This annual subject guide, presented in several volumes, has a subject heading called "Baseball" and various subheadings such as "Biography," "History," and "Juvenile Literature." It will tell you what books are "in print," that is, available for purchase by libraries and individuals.
2. *Cumulative Book Index*. 1928-1999. New York: H.W. Wilson, 1933-present. This annual author-title-subject index of books published in English anywhere

in the world ceased publication at the end of 1999. All entries are in a single alphabetical list with each book's author entry being the most complete. *Cumulative Book Index* is indispensable for finding books no longer in print and consequently not listed in Bowker's (see 1 above). For books prior to 1928, see *The United States Catalog*, 4th ed. (H.W. Wilson, 1928), a two-volume list of all books in print on January 1, 1928.

3. ***Book Review Digest***. 1905-present. New York: H.W. Wilson, 1905-present. Published monthly and later bound into annual volumes, *Book Review Digest* offers condensed critical reviews about books in all fields. A subject and title index appears in each annual volume, and a cumulative index is published every five years.

4. ***Book Review Index***. 1965-present. Detroit: Gale Research, 1965-present. Although *Book Review Index* lacks the summaries of book reviews found in *Book Review Digest* (see 3 above), it locates reviews in approximately twice as many periodicals.

5. ***The Readers' Guide to Periodical Literature***. 1900-present. New York: H.W. Wilson, 1905-present. Approximately 180 well-known general-interest magazines, including *Sport* and *Sports Ilustrated*, are indexed in the *Readers' Guide*. Softcover issues appear once or twice a month and are later combined and bound into yearly volumes. For material published before 1900, see *Poole's Index to Periodical Literature*, reprint, 6 vols. (Peter Smith, 1963).

6. ***The New York Times Index***. 1851-present. New York: New York *Times*, 1913-present. (Early *Indexes* reproduced by R.R. Bowker.) A subject index to America's newspaper of record, the *Times Index* is useful for locating material in other newspapers because it supplies dates the researcher may not know.

7. ***Personal Name Index to The New York Times Index***, 1851-1974, 22 vols. Succasunna, NJ: Roxbury Data Interface, 1976; 1975-1996, annual supplements. Verdi, NV: Roxbury Data Interface, 1976-1997. It is easier to find individual names in this index than in *The New York Times Index* (see 6 above) because in the *Times Index* names may appear under other headings, such as "Obituaries."

8. ***Biography Index***. New York: H.W. Wilson, 1946-present. This index covers biographical articles from about 2,000 popular and scholarly serials as well as book-length biographies and chapters in collective biographies. An index to professions and occupations in each volume contains a section on baseball.

9. ***Dictionary of American Biography***. 20 volumes plus 7 supplements. New York: Scribner, 1928-1981. A monumental source of information on Americans no longer living, the *DAB* contains 17,656 articles in all, about fifty of which deal with people who had some direct connection with baseball.

10. *American National Biography*. 24 volumes. New York: Oxford University Press, 1999. Essays on 17,450 men and women from all eras and all walks of American life. A comprehensive and inclusive new project distinct from the *DAB*.

11. *Current Biography*. 1940-present. New York: H.W. Wilson, 1940-present. This monthly reference service offers readable, informative profiles of people in the news, including sports figures. Annual bound volumes appear with an index.

Newspapers and Microfilm

Many libraries keep the local newspaper and other newspapers, often temporarily in hard copy and perhaps permanently in microform. Hard copy of newspapers has a certain attraction—it is easy on the eyes and gives the reader a "feel" for the period—but microforms (microfilm and microfiche) stand up much better to time and handling. Baseball researchers should be prepared to read microfilm and to learn how to use microfilm readers and reader-printers.

How do you find out which newspapers are available in microform? The standard source for this information is *Newspapers in Microform*, found in many libraries. This book will tell you if a newspaper is available in microform, but it cannot tell you which libraries hold the microform edition. Don't ever expect to find, for example, a list of all the libraries that hold *The Sporting News* on microfilm.

Indexes to newspapers are few and far between, but remember that *The New York Times Index* may be all you need to find material by date in any newspaper. Of course, if you are looking for feature stories not keyed to certain events or dates, then an index is certainly helpful. If the newspaper you are searching does not have an index, you might try contacting the newspaper itself. The paper's library may be willing to search its morgue or clipping file for you, perhaps for a fee.

One important point: Just as you shouldn't be intimidated by a large library, neither should you be scared by microfilm or microfilm readers. They're in the library for you to use, not to frighten you away. There's a first time for everything. Just tell the librarian exactly what newspaper and what dates you want to see, and if necessary, ask for help to get the machine working. Microfilm readers and reader-printers get lots of use. They break down frequently and often develop quirks. Librarians know their equipment and should be glad to make you feel comfortable.

Interlibrary Loan

If the book you want to read or the newspaper you want to examine is not available in your local library, you have another option in the Interlibrary Loan System (ILL). Using this fantastic service, researchers can ask their local libraries to borrow material from any library that participates in the system. Here are a few pointers about the interlibrary loan system...

1. In order for you to use ILL, your library must be a participant.
2. You must belong to the library (have a card) where you submit the ILL request.
3. Don't expect ILL libraries to lend everything. You can get many books and lots of microfilm, but you probably won't get current titles and best sellers, current reference books or rare books. You won't get magazines either, but you may be able to get photocopies of magazine articles.
4. You don't need to know which library has the item you want. The system will find it for you.
5. If you borrow books through ILL, you can charge them out and take them home. But if you borrow microfilm, you will have to view it at your local library.
6. Processing ILL requests often takes several weeks. But if you need a particular item, the wait will be worth it.

THREE SPECIAL LIBRARIES AND ARCHIVES

Despite all the help local libraries can provide to both new and experienced baseball researchers, there is really no substitute for being able to travel to one or more of the major institutions that specialize in baseball and sports information. Serious baseball researchers planning major projects should certainly decide whether their work can be completed successfully without visiting the National Baseball Hall of Fame Library in Cooperstown, New York. Alternatively, or perhaps additionally, researchers should consider visiting the archives of *The Sporting News* in St. Louis, Missouri, or the library of the Amateur Athletic Foundation of Los Angeles, California. Here are thumbnail sketches of these three institutions. Their addresses and phone numbers are available at the end of this chapter:

The National Baseball Hall of Fame Library, founded in 1939, has as its mission collecting, organizing, and preserving the complete history of baseball as recorded in all media formats for the use of fans and researchers. Located in the A. Bartlett Giamatti Research Center, the library is open to the public, but appointments are suggested.

The Library contains the most extensive collection of library and archival materials devoted exclusively to baseball. Holdings include books, periodicals, newspapers, clipping files, baseball guides, team publications, player contract cards, day-by-day statistics, and an array of archival materials. The Photograph Department contains over 400,000 images of players, teams, stadiums, events, and miscellaneous subjects. The Film, Video, and Recorded Sound Department contains thousands of hours of moving image and sound recordings, including interviews, game highlights, television and radio broadcasts, animation, and music.

The Archives of *The Sporting News*, established in 1986, has as its primary purpose supporting the staff of The Sporting News Publishing Company by collecting and main-

by Rick Bradley / Oral History Committee

Here are a few tips on making your oral histories as easy and successful as possible.

1. **Phone for an interview.** Two or three weeks in advance, call the player you would like to interview, explain who you are and what you'd like to do. Letters are less effective because they get misplaced or thrown out with autograph requests. If the player says "yes," set up a date, time, and place for the interview.

2. **Follow up with a letter as a reminder.** Include your phone number. I once flew to Little Rock, Arkansas, to see Willis Hudlin, only to learn that Willis and his wife were in Mississippi, visiting Mrs. Hudlin's seriously ill brother. Willis couldn't call me because I hadn't sent him the follow-up letter.

3. **Research the player's record before the interview.** Your ballplayer will be a better interview if he sees that you know your stuff. When looking for the playing records of most (if not all) ballplayers, both major and minor league, you need to look no further than SABR member Ray Nemec. Ray, who has spent many years compiling statistics, asks for $1 per player requested.

4. **Outline the questions you intend to ask.** You can obtain a general outline for player interviews from the Chair of the Oral History Committee—that's me at present —who can also provide you with lists of ballplayers and ex-ballplayers in your area.

5. **Be a good listener.** I've missed quite a few obvious follow-up questions during interviews because I spent too much time staring at the next question in my outline and not enough time listening to what was being said to me. Don't let this happen to you.

Norman Macht, long-time Chair of the Oral History Committee, hosted a forty-five-minute interviewing seminar at the 1993 SABR convention in San Diego. A copy of this informative seminar on cassette tape is available from me upon request.

Last, you need very little equipment to record your oral histories. I have both a tape recorder-with-microphone that plugs into the wall and a hand-held tape recorder for those places where an extension cord will not reach an outlet. Blank tapes from any of the major manufacturers will suffice. Remember to advance the cassette tape five to ten seconds on each side before beginning the recording phase. This assures that all of your interview will be included on the tape. And remember to begin all interviews with the following: name of the interviewer, name of interviewee, the current date, the location of the interview, and if the tape is being made for SABR, state this as well. Good luck!

taining materials relevant to the production of the company's weekly magazine and other products. In addition, the archives staff provides reference and research services to the public on a "by appointment" basis.

The holdings of the archives concentrate on the "Big Six" sports covered by *The Sporting News*: baseball, college and professional football, college and professional basketball, and hockey. The collection includes a 6,000-volume sports library, publications of the company, selected periodicals, team media guides, microfilm, clipping files on individuals and subjects, biographical questionnaires, player contract cards, and a photo collection of over 600,000 images.

The Amateur Athletic Foundation Library, housed in the Paul Ziffren Sports Resource Center, covers virtually all aspects of amateur and professional sport with information on the historical, social, and economic implications of sport as well as materials about athletic techniques, training methods, sports medicine, and coaching. The library is open to the public, but prospective visitors are urged to write or call ahead in order to avoid conflicts with special events.

The library's holdings include books, microforms, videos, periodicals, and photos. The strength of the collection is its coverage of the Olympic Games, but it also includes nearly complete runs of *The Sporting News* and *Sports Illustrated*, team media guides, World Series programs, the sports section of the Los Angeles *Times* dating back to the 1930s, and various other materials related to baseball. (SABR's Allan Roth Chapter, in fact, meets at the Ziffren Center.)

Two Other Institutions:

The Library of Congress is a truly immense place, but don't let its size frighten you. Anyone who has done research there will tell you that it is remarkably easy to use. Some baseball researchers, in fact, like Paul Dickson, do most of their work there.

What resources does LC offer to baseball researchers who can spend some time in Washington, D.C.? Joseph Puccio's "Baseball Research Resources at the Library of Congress," a four-page overview, is available from the SABR Research Papers Collection. As Puccio points out, LC has a comprehensive collection of books, both fiction and non-fiction; thousands of American newspapers; many periodicals; the Branch Rickey Papers, and baseball materials in many other formats—prints and photographs, music, motion pictures, and recorded sound.

The best way to obtain additional information about the library's holdings and the services it provides is to visit the LC Web site (www.loc.gov). Some researchers may feel more comfortable writing to the library, but the Web site is truly easier and quicker, and it contains a wealth of information. Once a researcher is in Washington, it is necessary to go to the library's Madison Building to obtain a Reader Identification Card, which is good for two years. This process requires a valid picture ID and can be time-consuming. Formal research orientation classes, taught by reference librarians and dealing with many aspects of using the library, are offered regularly.

The Genealogical Library of The Church of Jesus Christ of Latter-Day Saints in Salt Lake City, Utah, contains the world's largest and most complete collection of genealogical information, some of which may be useful to baseball researchers doing biographical research. Branch libraries throughout the United States—650 of them—have catalogs that list the main library's holdings, most of which can be obtained through the branches.

SABR's Archives

In 1998, SABR arranged for the Western Reserve Historical Society in Cleveland to become the depository for SABR's archives and research collections. Among the materials available for research at WRHS are:

- more than 2,500 books, including SABR's own publications plus runs of the Spalding and Reach guides, *The Sporting News Baseball Guide* and *The Baseball Register*;
- microfilm of *The Sporting News*, *Sporting Life*, *Baseball Magazine*, and the Albert Spalding Papers housed at the New York Public Library;
- several theses and dissertations;
- the SABR-Ottoson Photo Archive (5,500 black-and-white wire service photos, mostly from the late 1920s to the mid-1940s);
- copies of two databases (SABR home run log, SABR biographical database);
- approximately 200 cassette recordings of oral interviews;
- several private collections donated to SABR (including the John Tattersall Papers, the Allan Roth Collection, the Willie George Collection, the Arnold Springer Collection, and the Keith Sutton Collection);
- various clippings files;
- research files donated by various SABR members;
- SABR's institutional archives.

Special Collections in Libraries

Several major libraries across the country hold significant baseball materials in their special collections departments. Among the most significant are the following:

- **Boston Public Library**, Print Collection, Dartmouth Street at Copley Square, Boston, MA 02117: McGreevey Baseball Collection, 225 photos and paintings, 1870-1914;
- **Cleveland Public Library**, Social Sciences Department, 325 Superior Avenue, Cleveland, OH 44114: Charles W. Mears Baseball Collection, Eugene Murdoch Collection, scrapbooks, and records;

- **Detroit Public Library**, Burton Historical Collection, 5201 Woodward Avenue, Detroit, MI 48202: Ernie Harwell Collection, materials on the Tigers, including twelve letterbooks, 1900-1912;
- **New York Public Library**, Manuscripts and Archives Division, Fifth Avenue and 42nd Street, New York, NY 10018: Albert G. Spalding Collection, including Spalding's own scrapbooks, the correspondence of Harry Wright, the letterbook and diaries of Henry Chadwick, scrapbooks, scorebooks and other materials from the Cincinnati Red Stockings, and club books and game books of the Knickerbocker Base Ball Club. The library has retired the use of these original materials because they are extremely fragile. Researchers can use the microfilm edition, which is also available for purchase (fifteen reels at $35 per reel). Other materials in the Spalding Collection were transferred to the General Research Division (books and pamphlets) and to the Art, Prints, and Photographs Division (photographs and drawings);
- **Pettigrew Museum Library**, Siouxland Heritage Museums, 131 North Duluth Avenue, Sioux Falls, SD 57104: Northern League baseball records;
- **Smithsonian Institution Libraries**, National Museum of American History Branch, Constitution Avenue at Tenth Street, NW, Washington, DC 20560: 2,000 baseball cards.

Other Archival Resources

No handbook of this length can do justice to the number and variety of institutions across the United States that hold archival materials and may have collections related to baseball. Researchers interested in doing advanced archival work should begin by consulting three sources: *Subject Collections*, published by R.R. Bowker; the *Directory of Special Libraries and Information Centers*, published by Gale Research; and the *National Union Catalog of Manuscript Collections*, published by the Library of Congress.

National Baseball Hall of Fame Library
25 Main Street, P.O. Box 590
Cooperstown, NY 13326

Research Center:(607) 547-0030
Photo Department: (607) 547-0377
Film/Video/Recordings Dept.:
(607) 547-0333
Fax: (607) 547-4094

www.baseballhalloffame.org/library

Archives, The Sporting News
10176 Corporate Square Dr., Ste. 200
St. Louis, MO 63132

Phone: (314) 993-7787 or 993-7777
Fax: (314) 997-0765
Email: archives@sportingnews.com

www.sportingnews.com/archives/research

Western Reserve Historical Society
10825 East Boulevard
University Circle
Cleveland, OH 44106

Phone: (216) 721-5722
Fax: (216) 721-0645
Email: reference@wrhs.org

www.wrhs.org

Amateur Athletic
Foundation Library
2141 West Adams Boulevard
Los Angeles, CA 90018

Phone: (323) 730-9696
Fax: (323) 730-0546
Email: library@aafla.org

www.aafla.org/library

National Reference Service
Library of Congress
101 Independence Avenue, SE
Washington, DC 20540-4720

www.loc.gov

Genealogical Library
Church of Jesus Christ
of Latter-Day Saints
35 North West Temple Street
Salt Lake City, UT 84150

Phone: (801) 240-2331

www.familysearch.org

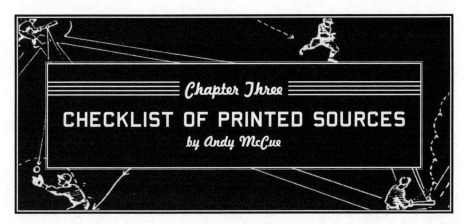

Chapter Three

CHECKLIST OF PRINTED SOURCES
by Andy McCue

In the dozen years since the first edition of *The Baseball Research Handbook* in 1987, there has been an explosion of books on baseball. At the end of 1986, there were approximately 12,000 baseball books. At the beginning of 2000, there are almost 18,000. The traditional book publishers, plus SABR, its members and fellow travelers have greatly expanded the material available to researchers. There have been foundation works—such as encyclopedias for the minor leagues, the Negro Leagues, and nineteenth-century baseball—as well as books on specific topics from the old (Cap Anson, the Philadelphia Athletics) to the new (women in baseball, Robin Yount). Areas rarely explored earlier, such as the business of baseball and the Latin American game, have been the beneficiaries of substantial new research and writing.

In such a universe of books, detailed descriptions are not possible, but this chapter seeks to introduce and briefly discuss central works in the major fields of interest to SABR researchers. Experienced researchers are likely to find little they aren't familiar with, although a concise refresher never hurts. And for most categories, especially such popular fields as biographies and team histories, the books chosen are merely representative of the genre. If a book is left out, that is not necessarily a reflection on its quality.

STARTING OUT: Bibliographies

The obvious place to start a list of books is with books of lists. Bibliographies remain critical in starting research. Because they are being replaced by computer-based sources (see Chapter 4), there is little new in this field in recent years.

There are two major bibliographies of baseball materials.

1. Grobani, Anton. *Guide to Baseball Literature*. Detroit: Gale Research Co., 1975, 363 pp.
2. Smith, Myron J., Jr. *Baseball: A Comprehensive Bibliography*. Jefferson, NC: McFarland & Co., 1986, 915pp. Supplement 1, McFarland & Co., 1993, 422pp. Supplement 2, McFarland & Co., 1998, 310 pp.

The best discussion of these two works remains Frank Phelps's article in the *SABR Bibliography Committee Newsletter*, 87-1, February 16, 1987, and his review in *The SABR Review of Books* of 1987. Because of the relative strengths and weaknesses that Phelps mentions, which are discussed briefly below, it is best to consult both books and the electronic resources, especially The Baseball Index, which are superseding them. (See Chapter 4, "Using the Computer for Baseball Research.)

Grobani's seminal bibliography lists nearly 3,000 works. Its strengths include a high level of accuracy, and the inclusion of areas such as early club constitutions, which are not included in Smith.

Its weaknesses are that it contains nothing published after 1972, does not contain any material from magazines or other journals, and is badly organized. (Frank Phelps of SABR's Bibliography Committee has produced an "Author Index to 'Guide to Baseball Literature,'" which is of immense help in using Grobani. The index is available through Len Levin's SABR Research Exchange (see below).

Smith is a professional bibliographer who has turned out works in a number of fields. His original 1986 baseball volume, containing some 21,251 entries, has been continued with supplements in 1993 (7,771 entries) and 1998 (5,167 entries). The publisher, McFarland, says an update, combining the three previous volumes and adding new material, is scheduled for publication in 2004.

The Smith volumes' strengths are the inclusion of thousands of magazine citations, including *Baseball Magazine*, *Sport*, *Sports Illustrated*, *Baseball Digest*, and *Inside Sports*, periodic updates, and its organization. It contains subject and author indexes which make it easier to navigate than Grobani. It also contains many academic dissertations.

Its weaknesses are incompleteness (Phelps found some 800 books included in the earlier Grobani volume which were not in Smith) and a tendency to errors. The errors range from the merely irritating (wrong page numbers for a magazine citation) to ludicrous (a book on the Texas Rangers which is about the law-enforcement organization).

Four other bibliographic works may be of some use:

3. Walker, Donald E., and B. Lee Cooper. *Baseball and American Culture: A Thematic Bibliography of Over 4,500 Works*. Jefferson, NC: McFarland & Co., 1995, 257 pp. Contains 4,627 references to books and articles. Many overlap Smith, but they are organized thematically ("Ethnic Diversity in Baseball," "Values Treasured by Americans," etc.) into twenty-five sections. The section themes focus on academic concerns.

4. Adomites, Paul D., comp. "The Essential Baseball Library," *The SABR Review of Books*, Volume II, 1987, pp. 9-19. This article contains fifty-seven books recommended by an all-star panel of SABR researchers as the core for any research library.

5. Shannon, Mike. *Diamond Classics: Essays on 100 of the Best Baseball Books Ever Published*. Jefferson, NC: McFarland & Co., 1989, 455 pp. Contains reviews of top baseball books.

6. McCue, Andy. *Baseball by the Books: A History and Complete Bibliography of Baseball Fiction*. Dubuque, IA: William C. Brown, 1991. 164 pp. The definitive bibliography of baseball fiction. Updated regularly by the author.

Baseball Encyclopedias

Since the appearance of the Macmillan *Baseball Encyclopedia* in 1969, the quality of baseball encyclopedias has improved quite significantly. Macmillan's was a marked improvement over earlier efforts, and today *Total Baseball* has broadened the definition of the genre.

7. Thorn, John, Pete Palmer, et al., eds. *Total Baseball, Sixth Edition: The Official Encyclopedia of Major League Baseball*. New York: Total Sports, 1999, 2,538 pp. Earlier editions were published by Warner Books (1st and 2nd), HarperPerennial (3rd), and Viking (4th and 5th). *Total Baseball* surged ahead of the competition because it is much closer to what we think of as an "encyclopedia." It is not limited to tabular data. In addition to the statistical material which has been the basis of baseball encyclopedias since they first appeared, *Total Baseball* contains essays on various areas of baseball history and interest. The topics range from baseball and the law to ballplayers who never existed to baseball movies to a history of top awards, such as the Most Valuable Player trophy. The authors are generally drawn from the top drawer of SABR researchers. The list of topics has changed from volume to volume, although such basic topics as the Negro Leagues and college baseball have been updated in each edition.

8. *The Baseball Encyclopedia*, Tenth edition, revised and updated. New York: Macmillan, 1996, 3,026 pp. Although Macmillan has decided to cease publishing the *Baseball Encyclopedia*, the book deserves a place on researchers' shelves for more than the sentimental value the Mac earned by being the first truly modern baseball encyclopedia in 1969. The 1969 edition remains the best single source for pitchers' batting statistics. The 8th edition (1990) was the first encyclopedia to list Negro League statistics, although it has been surpassed by *The Negro Leagues Book* (see #100). The 9th edition (1993) contains standings and an all-time roster for the All-American Girls Professional Baseball League. This latest edition contains the most up-to-date player-by-player summary of trades. At press time, IDG Books is planning an 11th edition for the fall of 2000.

9. Neft, David S., Richard M. Cohen, et al., eds. *The Sports Encyclopedia: Baseball*, 19th edition. New York: St. Martin's Press, 1999, 752 pp. While *Total Baseball* is organized by individual statistics and topical essays, *The Sports Encyclopedia: Baseball* is organized by seasons. It contains full rosters and basic statistical data as well as an essay about each season's pennant race. For the researcher interested in approaching the game this way, or in watching statistical progression over the seasons, Neft and Cohen's long-lived annual may have more to offer than *Total Baseball*. Contains no nineteenth-century material.

BASEBALL NEWSPAPERS AND MAGAZINES: *Current Newspapers*

Daily newspapers in major league cities, especially those such as the Boston *Globe*, the New York *Times*, the Dallas *Morning News*, and the Los Angeles *Times*, which cover baseball on a national basis, remain an unparalleled source of research material. In addition, while nothing exists to rival the pre-1970 *Sporting News* as a source, a number of newspapers, mostly weeklies, cover the sport.

10. *The Sporting News*. 1886-present. St. Louis: C.C. Spink Publishing Co. While *The Sporting News* has de-emphasized baseball over the years, it still reports weekly on the sport and its teams. Microfilm of *TSN*, available from the SABR Lending Library for the issues from March 1886 through December 1963, is an invaluable source of information on baseball events. Full box score coverage appeared through 1991. There is also Kehde, Ned, ed. *Index to The Sporting News*, Evanston: IL: John Gordon Burke, 1998, 518 pp. This is limited to the years 1975-1995 and covers only proper nouns—mostly names of individuals, clubs, and leagues.

11. *USA Today Baseball Weekly*, 1991-present. Arlington, VA: Gannett Publishing Co. *Baseball Weekly* is much more like *The Sporting News* of old with its exclusive emphasis on baseball. But it lacks the in-depth coverage that made *TSN* great, and its high consciousness of fantasy baseball orients many articles in that direction. It is written more for the fan than for the baseball insider and thus is less valuable to the researcher. However, it has always carried full major league box scores and transactions and remains the only printed source for them except for daily newspapers.

12. *Baseball America*. 1981-present. Durham, NC: American Sports Publishing. *Baseball America* concentrates on minor league baseball, but from the perspective of major league player development. It has excellent columnists and a thoughtful approach to issues that affect the minors. It began as a monthly and steadily increased its publishing frequency over the years, currently producing an issue every two weeks.

Defunct Newspapers

The Sporting News is the only survivor of three weekly newspapers that covered baseball heavily in the nineteenth century. The other two can be excellent sources of research for the years in which they were published.

13. *Sporting Life*. 1883-1917, 1922-1926. Name changed to *Sport Life* in 1924. *Sporting Life* was a very serious competitor for baseball news in its first thirty-four years of existence, the period when Francis C. Richter was the editor. The issues from April 1883 through February 1917 are available on microfilm through the SABR Lending Library.

14. New York *Clipper*. 1853-1924. The New York *Clipper* was the first publication to devote a great deal of space to baseball, along with the theater, the paper's first and last love. Baseball coverage was much heavier in the nineteenth century than in the publication's later years.

Current Magazines

Springtime usually sees an explosion of annual baseball magazines, the most enduring of which are *Street and Smith's Baseball Yearbook* (1941-present, published under slightly different titles in earlier years) and *The Sporting News Baseball Yearbook* (1982-present). These magazines are generally built around rosters, schedules, profiles of current stars, analyses of the most recent season, and predictions for the coming season. They can be an excellent source for understanding the expectations for a given season. Such general sports magazines as *Sport* (1946-present) and *Sports Illustrated* (1954-present) also provide baseball coverage during the season.

15. *Baseball Digest*. 1942-present. Evanston, IL: Century Publishing Co. The monthly *Baseball Digest* has always been a somewhat breezy publication, very oriented to the fan. The staples of the magazine are profiles and other material about individual players. It contains both original articles and reprints from newspapers around the country, as well as rosters and statistical tables.

16. *The Baseball Research Journal*, 1972-present, and *The National Pastime*, 1982-present. Cleveland: The Society for American Baseball Research. These two publications of SABR contain the research output of its members. In general, these publications have appeared annually, although *The National Pastime* appeared twice in 1985. While the material in the journals is basically similar, *The Baseball Research Journal* is a more nuts-and-bolts product and includes articles of statistical analysis. *The National Pastime* generally seeks a wider audience, a readership beyond SABR. Some *TNP* issues have been primarily pictorial. The Spring 1988 edition of *TNP* is devoted com-

pletely to a biography of Napoleon Lajoie—a biography that remains the most complete work available on the Hall of Famer. Many issues are still available, either originals or reprints, through the University of Nebraska Press, P.O. Box 880484, Lincoln, NE 68588-0484. Both publications are completely indexed through The Baseball Index.

17. Kirwin, Bill, ed. *Nine: A Journal of Baseball History and Social Policy Perspectives*. Toronto: Canadian Scholars Press, 1992-present. *Nine* is an academic publication with feature articles and numerous book reviews twice a year. There is a heavy emphasis on literature and sociological topics.

18. Wayman, Joseph M., ed. *Grandstand Baseball Annual*. Downey, CA: Joseph M. Wayman, 1985-present. An annual compilation of baseball research that has won numerous SABR awards. Wayman and his authors have done ground-breaking work in a number of areas—establishing turn-of-the-century pitching records, for example.

Defunct Baseball Magazines

Baseball magazines have come and gone like rookies in April, and many can provide useful material. One, however, stuck long enough to merit special mention.

19. Lane, F.C., ed. *Baseball Magazine*. 1908-1957; 1964-1965. Boston, New York, and Washington, DC: Baseball Magazine Co. From its inception until the early 1950s, when it fell on hard times, *Baseball Magazine* was a major publication. Especially in the years from the early 1910s to the mid-1930s, when it was edited by F.C. Lane, the monthly magazine produced some of the more thoughtful articles on the game. The SABR Lending Library has the issues from November 1910 through 1954 on microfilm.

Baseball Guides and Registers

Guidebooks have been produced since 1860. Over the years, they have contained various things, from league constitutions and rules to instructional material. The underlying theme, however, has always been a review of the previous season with a fairly thorough statistical compilation. For the nineteenth century, they are a primary source. The titles are not exact for every year. The word "official" often seems to come and go, but the titles below are those by which the books are generally known.

Here is one highly useful reference tool for the guides:

20. Spalding, John. *John Spalding's Guide to Baseball Guides, Record Books & Registers, 1869-1995*. San Jose, CA: John Spalding, 1996, 64 pp. This indexes longer articles and statistical features in 270 guides and registers.

21. *The Sporting News Official Baseball Guide*. 1942-present. St. Louis: The Sporting News. Major features include a review of the previous season, full major league statistics for that season, minor league statistics arranged by league, and schedules and rosters for the current season. Current editions include day-by-day won-lost records for the previous season.

22. *The Sporting News Official Baseball Register*. 1940-present. St. Louis: The Sporting News. The *Register* contains players' career records with year-by-year statistics, including minor league records, for all active major league players and managers. In various years, managers, coaches, umpires, and former stars, especially that year's Hall of Fame inductees, have had their full records included as well. Frank Phelps's *Index to The Sporting News Baseball Registers, 1940-1995* (SABR Bibliography Committee, 1996) lists all who have appeared in *TSN Registers* and in what years. For establishing the full records of players who returned to the minors after their major league careers, this resource is invaluable. It is available from the SABR office. In addition, Bob McConnell produced SABR Research Guide #3, *Baseball Register: Overview & Index to Features & "Former Stars" Type Records* in 1986. It indexes the profiles and topical features that ran in many earlier *TSN Registers*. This is available through the SABR Research Exchange.

23. *The National League Green Book*. 1934-present. New York: National League of Professional Baseball Clubs.

24. *The American League Red Book*. 1937-present. New York: American League of Professional Baseball Clubs. Unlike most record books and guides, the Green and Red books look ahead. While they do have statistics, they are most valuable for information on umpires and schedules.

25. *The Baseball America Almanac*. 1983-present. Durham, NC: Baseball America. Similar to major league guides, but much more emphasis on minor league developments. Statistics are broken down by major league organization rather than by league. From 1983 through 1987, it was known as the *Baseball America Statistics Report*.

26. *USA Today Baseball Weekly Almanac*. 1992-present. New York: Total Sports. 1992-1996 editions published by Hyperion; 1997-1998 editions by Henry Holt. Same basic material as *TSN* Guides. Also includes salary information, disabled-list data, and franchise statistical records.

27. *Who's Who in Professional Baseball*. New York: Who's Who in Baseball. 1912, 1916-present, 352 pp. Similar to the *TSN Register* in both content and organization. It is not as complete but has hung on because of lower price,

smaller size, and a newsdealer distribution network. Published by *Baseball Magazine* from its inception through 1957.

28. ***Super Register***. Durham, NC: Baseball America, 1998-present. Basic format is the same as *The Sporting News Register*. There are fewer columns of statistical information on each player, but the book does contain all players in both the minors and the majors.

29. Hoie, Bob, and Carlos Bauer, compilers. ***The Historical Register***. San Diego: Baseball Press Books, 1998, 446 pp. Presents the records of 750 of the top players in baseball history. The unique feature of this book is that it pursues the players' minor league careers after they left the majors, through semipro leagues, independent leagues, and outlaw leagues. Regularly updated.

Defunct Guides and Registers

30. ***Beadle's Dime Base-Ball Player***. 1860-1862, 1864-1881. Henry Chadwick, ed. New York: Beadle & Co. The first guide, *Beadle's* contains rules, records, elementary statistics, discussions of notable games of the previous season, and lists of delegates to various baseball meetings. It set the template from which all future guides evolved. It died when Chadwick left for the more successful Spalding Guides series.

31. ***DeWitt's Base-Ball Guide***. 1868-1885. New York: Robert M. DeWitt. Very similar to *Beadle's*, but also contains a model club constitution and bylaws, instructions on scorekeeping, coaching hints, and umpiring tips. Averages first appeared in *DeWitt's* 1872 edition.

32. ***Spalding's Official Base Ball Guide***. 1878-1939. New York: A.G. Spalding & Bros., 1878-1893. New York: American Sports Publishing Co., 1894-1939. During its heyday, Spalding's was the king of the guides. From 1908-1924, it only superficially covered the minor leagues. That information was transferred to the publication below. *Spalding's Guide* was the official publication of the National League. In the late 1980s and early 1990s, Ralph Horton reprinted the Spalding Guides, 1876-1905.

33. ***Spalding's Official Base Ball Record***. 1908-1924. New York: American Sports Publishing Co. Includes the minor league records noted above, as well as major league, college, and semipro statistics and recaps.

34. ***Reach's Official Base Ball Guide***. 1883-1939. Philadelphia: A.J. Reach, 1883-1927. Philadelphia: A.J. Reach, Wright & Ditson, 1928-1934. New York: American Sports Publishing Co., 1935-1939. In content highly similar to *Spalding's*, although more comprehensive. *Reach's Guide* started out as the official publication of the American Association (then a major league) and

switched to the American League in 1902. Ralph Horton reprinted the 1883-1905 Reach Guides in the late 1980s and early 1990s.

35. *Spalding-Reach Official Baseball Guide*. 1940-1941. New York: American Sports Publishing Co. Combined successor to the Spalding and Reach guides.

36. *1943 Baseball; Official Baseball 1945-1946*. Chicago: Office of the Baseball Commissioner, 1943. New York: A.S. Barnes & Co., 1945-1946. With the demise of the Spalding-Reach guides, *The Sporting News* stepped into the market. But it was not official. The Commissioner's office put out a 1943 guide and canonized A.S. Barnes for the 1945 and 1946 editions. The 1945 edition covers both the 1943 and 1944 seasons.

Record Books

The fascination with baseball's firsts, mosts, and longests has existed as long as the game's written record. Hundreds of record books have been published over the years, but only those that are constantly updated have any continuing research value. There are two annual publications these days:

37. Carter, Craig, ed. *The Sporting News Complete Baseball Record Book, 1986-present*. St. Louis: The Sporting News, 1999, 576 pp. This volume subsumes the material that The Sporting News formerly published as *The Baseball Dope Book* (1942, 1948-1985), *One for the Book* (1949-1971), and *Official World Series Records* (1953-1985). An earlier version, known as *The Sporting News Record Book* was published from 1909-1941.

38. Siwoff, Seymour, ed. *The Book of Baseball Records. 1926-present*. New York: Seymour Siwoff-Elias Sports Bureau, 1999, 398 pp. This publication began as *The Little Red Book of Baseball*, the title it used until 1971. This book has, until recent years, been better at updating records than *The Sporting News* book, which has, however, improved. While these two standard baseball record books (#37 and #38) are similar, *The Sporting News* series is generally easier to find, has larger print, and appears to have a few more records, especially World Series records, than the Elias book. It also often comes out a bit earlier in the spring.

SPECIAL SABR PUBLICATIONS: *Committee Newsletters*

All SABR committees are required to publish a newsletter at least once a year. These vary in usefulness for research. The Statistical Analysis newsletter, for example, contains original research. The newsletters for Negro Leagues and Ballparks have no research articles, but are full of references to newspaper and magazine articles, as well as other items that might help a researcher.

Research Guides

The Bibliography Committee has published fifteen research guides which can be a great help. Some have been mentioned already. Here are the others, with the year of publication in parentheses.

> **#1** – Baseball Figures in *Current Biography* (1986).
> **#2** – Index to Professional Baseball Figures in *Who's Who in American Sports* (1986).
> **#4** – Indexes to Stars and Authors in *Baseball Stars of 1950, 1953-1975* (1986).
> **#6** – Baseball Figures in *Dictionary of American Biography* (1987).
> **#7** – Overview and Pre-1948 Player Index for *Who's Who in Baseball* (1987).
> **#8** – Index to *Daguerreotypes of Great Stars of Baseball*, all editions (1987).
> **#9** – (Library) Collections on the History of American Baseball.
> **#10** – Baseball in History Journals.
> **#11** – *Daguerreotypes* Published in *The Sporting News*, a Checklist.
> **#12** – *Leaves from a Fan's Scrapbook* Published in *The Sporting News*.
> **#13** – *The Dope Book*, 1942, 1948-1985, a Subject Index.
> **#14** – Box Scores of Major and Minor Leagues in *Sporting Life* and *The Sporting News*, a Chronology (1985).

Research guides are available through the SABR Research Exchange (see below).

Baseball Rules

In the early years, rules were often included in the guides. Currently, the best publication is *Official Baseball Rules*, published annually by *The Sporting News* since 1950. This book is updated, with new rules or rules changes indicated by underlining.

Other Reference Works

The research done by SABR members and the growth of the baseball market have fostered basic reference works that can be of great value. Where possible, as with *The Negro Leagues Book*, these are discussed in the more specific topic section below. Here are some others:

> **39.** Dickson, Paul, ed. ***The New Dickson Baseball Dictionary***. San Diego: Harcourt Brace & Co., 1999, 579 pp. A highly useful, annotated list of baseball terms, their origins and meanings and references to their first appearance in print. A must. This book is an update of the 1989 original from Facts on File.

40. Light, Jonathan Fraser, ed. *The Cultural Encyclopedia of Baseball*. Jefferson, NC: McFarland & Co., 1997, 888 pp. Entries cover a wide, wide range of topics (no statistics), from players and ballparks to salaries and groundskeepers. Some are humorous, many are revealing. The book draws on an enormous range of resources.

41. Okkonen, Mark, ed. *Baseball Uniforms of the Twentieth Century*. New York: Sterling Publishing, 1991 and 1993, 278 pp. The 1993 paperback updates the material and corrects some errors in the original. The definitive work on uniforms, with drawings illustrating how each team's uniforms changed from year to year.

42. Stang, Mark, and Linda Harkness. *Baseball by the Numbers: A Guide to the Uniform Numbers of Major League Teams*. Lanham, MD: Scarecrow Press, 1997, 1,125 pp. The ultimate guide to uniform numbers. Lists them by team, by year, and by number. Inclusive through the 1992 season.

43. McConnell, Bob, and David Vincent, eds. *SABR Presents The Home Run Encyclopedia*. New York: Macmillan, 1996, 1,311 pp. Covers 1876-1995 seasons and lists all home runs by batter, with breakdowns such as home/road.

44. Smith, Curt. *Voices of the Game*. New York: Simon & Schuster, 1992, 623pp. Not a reference book *per se*, but a history of baseball broadcasting with extensive reference to Smith's interviews with the announcers. This is an update of the 1987 original from Diamond Communications of South Bend, Indiana. Many of the interviews are reproduced at greater length in Smith's *The Storytellers* (New York: Macmillan, 1995, 278 pp.).

45. Erickson, Hal. *Baseball in the Movies: A Comprehensive Reference, 1915-1991*. Jefferson, NC: McFarland & Co., 1992, 402 pp. Covers baseball feature films (no instructionals, World Series highlight reels, or similar historical material). Long plot summaries combined with basic information and some discussion of a film's context in both movies and baseball.

46. Dinhofer, Shelly Mehlman. *The Art of Baseball*. New York: Harmony Books, 1990, 159 pp. Coffee-table-sized book filled with reproductions of all kinds of baseball art, some with historic interest and others providing fodder for the more sociologically inclined.

47. Smalling, R.J. "Jack." *The Baseball Autograph Collector's Handbook*. Durham, NC: Baseball America, 1999. This book was previously known as the *Sports Americana Baseball Address List*, published by Edgewater Book Co. in Cleveland through nine editions. It is valuable to researchers because it contains addresses for old ballplayers, umpires, coaches, and managers, who can be contacted for interviews.

48. Thompson, S.C., ed. Revised 1973 edition by Pete Palmer. ***All-Time Rosters of Major League Baseball Clubs***. New York: A.S. Barnes, 1973. 723 pp. If you are looking for all-time rosters by clubs, this remains the most comprehensive source, despite becoming increasingly out of date. *The Sports Encyclopedia: Baseball* covers all years, including those after this volume.

49. Chronologies: Between 1979 and 1984, Leisure Press and Stein and Day published a series of major league team chronologies, such as *This Date in New York Yankees History* (New York: Stein and Day, 1983) and *Day by Day in New York Yankees History* (New York: Leisure Press, 1983). Chronologies were published for each of the sixteen classic franchises except the Athletics and the Senators/Twins. The Yankees and Browns/Orioles are the only teams with books in both series. The only expansion teams with their own chronologies are the Mets, Expos, and Brewers, the latter by Everson House of Appleton, Wisconsin, in 1987.

Book Reviews

Book reviews of baseball books can be hard to find. Several sources are *Nine* (see current baseball magazines above), the *Elysian Fields Quarterly* (2034 Marshall Ave., St. Paul, MN 55104), and the newsletter of SABR's Bibliography Committee. The short-lived *SABR Review of Books* (annually 1986-1990) and its successor *The Cooperstown Review: A Forum of Baseball Literary Opinion* (1993-1994) are also good sources.

BOOKS ON BROAD CATEGORIES: General Histories

There are many histories of the game, dating back to Alfred Spink's *The National Game*, published in 1910, and ranging from picture books for children on up. For research purposes, however, the choices are much more limited. There are two three-volume histories, both somewhat academic in their approach, and two more recent efforts to encapsulate the game in one volume.

50. Seymour, Harold. ***Baseball: The Early Years***, New York: Oxford University Press, 1960, 373 pp. (covers origins to 1903), ***Baseball: The Golden Years***, Oxford University Press, 1971, 492 pp. (covers 1903 to 1930) and ***Baseball: The People's Game***, Oxford University Press, 1990, 639 pp. (Covers non-professional baseball, with topics from town teams to prison teams).

51. Voigt, David. ***American Baseball: From Gentleman's Sport to the Commissioner System***, Norman, OK: University of Oklahoma Press, 1966, 336 pp., ***American Baseball: From the Commissioners to Continental Expansion***, University of Oklahoma Press, 1970, 350 pp. and ***American Baseball: From Postwar Expansion to the Electronic Age***, University of

Oklahoma Press, 1983, 414 pp. Seymour's series was unfortunately cut short by his death in 1992, limiting his chronological coverage of professional baseball to the period before 1930. His series is undoubtedly the most thorough.

Voigt's books, while not as detailed as Seymour's, cover the major themes and weave them together well. Their coverage of the period between 1930 and 1982 is a major plus for someone looking to review more recent history.

52. James, Bill. *The Historical Baseball Abstract*. New York: Villard Books, 1985, 721 pp. (A 1987 paperback from Villard updates the original.) James's *Abstract* takes a more individual path than Seymour's or Voigt's narrative histories. Highly readable, it features James's iconoclastic approach to baseball's perceived wisdom and his statistical expertise. The author has a thorough knowledge of the basic trends throughout the game's history.

53. Rader, Benjamin. *Baseball*. Urbana, IL: University of Illinois Press, 1992, 231 pp. Rader attempts to synthesize all the best research on the game into a one-volume history suitable for university courses. While obviously less detailed than either Seymour or Voigt, it serves its purpose well.

54. Sullivan, Dean, ed. *Early Innings: A Documentary History of Baseball, 1825-1908*. Lincoln, NE: University of Nebraska Press, 1995, 312 pp. and *Middle Innings: A Documentary History of Baseball, 1900-1948*. University of Nebraska Press, 1998, 238 pp. First-hand documents or accounts of important baseball events. A third volume, covering the years 1945-1969, is scheduled for publication in 2001.

League and Team Histories

55. Allen, Lee. *The National League Story*. New York: Hill and Wang, 1961. Rev. ed., 1965, 293 pp.

56. Allen, Lee. *The American League Story*. New York: Hill and Wang, 1962, 242 pp. These remain the standard league histories. Allen's role at the Hall of Fame helped make these the official histories and his style makes them very readable.

57. Pietrusza, David. *Major Leagues: The Formation, Sometimes Absorption and Mostly Inevitable Demise of 18 Professional Baseball Organizations, 1871 to Present*. Jefferson, NC: McFarland & Co., 1991, 375 pp. This volume is most useful for Pietrusza's intelligent treatment of leagues other than the better-known survivors.

Team histories have been one of the most active areas in the explosion of baseball books over the past couple of decades. Virtually every team has had multiple volumes written about it. Depending on your needs, you will want to explore different types of team histories. You should also give consideration to team publications, such as yearbooks and media guides. Media guides started as roster books in the 1930s, and yearbooks first appeared in the late 1940s. Over the years, especially as the 1970s progressed, they contained more and more information—team records, minor league players, profiles, and other data. Some general works:

58. Bjarkman, Peter C., ed. *Encyclopedia of Major League Baseball Team Histories: The National League* (548 pp.) and *The American League* (575 pp.). Both were published by Meckler Publishing in Westport, CT, in 1991. Both books collect historical essays on each franchise, most of the essays by noted SABR researchers. All contain annotated bibliographies.

59. Filichia, Peter. *Professional Baseball Franchises: From the Abbeville Athletics to the Zanesville Indians*. New York: Facts on File, 1993, 290pp. A useful quick reference to franchises in both the minors and the majors. Listed by city with years, leagues, and nicknames.

60. Dewey, Donald, and Nicholas Acocella. *The Ball Clubs*. New York: HarperPerennial, 1996, 604 pp. This is an update of the *Encyclopedia of Major League Baseball Teams*, which HarperCollins published in 1993. It covers all major league teams, even those that barely made a ripple. Each entry contains team name, league(s) it was in, its all-time record, ballpark(s), and season-by-season records. It also contains a narrative history that can run from less than a page for a short-lived franchise such as the American Association's 1884 Richmond Virginians to twenty-one pages for a team such as the Detroit Tigers.

Team Histories: The Long-term Narrative

The classics of this genre are the team histories of the original sixteen franchises published by G.P. Putnam's Sons between 1943 and 1955. These are detailed narratives going back to the team's founding, with summaries of performance and major changes year by year. Typical is Frederick Lieb's *The Baltimore Orioles: The History of a Colorful Team* (1955, 246 pp.), which also contains considerable material on the 1890s Orioles of the National League and the International League Orioles. These books were done by sportswriters, and several have problems with misspelled names or other factual errors. They were published without indexes, but, to make their content accessible to researchers, indexes have been created by SABR's Bibliography Committee and are available through the SABR Research Exchange (see below).

Unfortunately, no series as organized as Putnam's has been produced in recent years, although some teams have been honored with excellent works:

61. Hynd, Noel. *The Giants of the Polo Grounds*. New York: Doubleday, 1988, 397 pp. This outshines the Putnam's volume on the Giants but does not extend to the San Francisco years.

62. Miller, James Edward. *The Baseball Business: Pursuing Pennants & Profits in Baltimore*. Chapel Hill, NC: University of North Carolina Press, 1990, 382 pp. Excellent at weaving in the team's relationship with the wider community and the business aspects of the game with the team's on-field performance. Does not deal with the franchise's pre-Baltimore years.

63. Torry, Jack. *Endless Summers: The Fall and Rise of the Cleveland Indians*. South Bend, IN: Diamond Communications, 1995, 303 pp. Updated in 1997 at 337 pp.

64. Harrigan, Patrick J. *The Detroit Tigers: Club and Community, 1945-1995*. Toronto: University of Toronto Press, 1997, 415 pp. Other teams, such as the Phillies, have not had a substantial update in this genre.

Team Histories: The Short-term Narrative

These cover a season (usually a pennant-winner) or a relatively short era for one team. Using the Mets as an example…

65. Breslin, Jimmy. *Can't Anybody Here Play This Game?* New York: Viking, 1963, 124 pp. A collection of anecdotes about the inept early years of this highly publicized expansion team.

66. Zimmerman, Paul D., and Dick Schaap. *The Year the Mets Lost Last Place*. New York: The World Publishing Co., 1969, 223 pp. When the Mets finally won it all in 1969, several books were produced about that season's team.

67. Lang, Jack, and Peter Simon. *The New York Mets: Twenty-Five Years of Baseball Magic*. New York: New York: Henry Holt and Co., 1987, 255 pp. When the 1986 team returned the franchise to World Series victory, the saga of the Mets was quickly updated.

68. Klapisch, Bob, and John Harper. *The Worst Team Money Could Buy: The Collapse of the New York Mets*. New York: Random House, 1993, 281 pp. This book deals with the collapse of the mid-1980s Mets in a welter of drugs and misplaced salaries.

Some other excellent examples of the short-term narrative:

69. Asinof, Eliot. *Eight Men Out: The Black Sox and the 1919 World Series*. New York: Holt, Rinehart and Winston, 1963, 302 pp. Still the starting point for researching the Black Sox scandal.

DOING BIOGRAPHICAL RESEARCH

by Bill Carle / Chair, Biographical Research Committee

The goal of the Biographical Research Committee is to establish accurate birth and death data for every player who has played in the major leagues since 1871, a total of over 15,000 players. Much of the research done by committee members is similar to the type of research done by a genealogist. The first step is usually to search through microfilm, old newspapers or magazines to find clues about the player, such as where he was born or where he was playing prior to his major league debut. The Baseball Hall of Fame Library in Cooperstown maintains a biographical file on each player. These files contain notes about each player's life.

Newspaper microfilm can be obtained through the Interlibrary Loan System with the assistance of your local librarian. Such magazines as *Sporting Life* and *The Sporting News* also contain clues and can be obtained on microfilm from the SABR Lending Library. Copies of current newspapers can often be found on the Web. There are a couple of sites where you can find URLs for newspapers. One is www.theslacks.com/news/usnp.html, and the other is www.philly.com/newslibrary.

Often, researchers need to write for birth or death certificates. Not all states send them freely to non-relatives, but the mailing address you will need for each state can be found in *The Vital Records Handbook* by Thomas Jay Kemp. Certain states maintain indexes to death records that are readily available either on the Web or at genealogical libraries. States that have indexes include California, Georgia, Idaho, Kentucky, Ohio, Oregon, Texas, Vermont, and Washington. Copies of wills may be obtained by writing the Hall of Records in the city where the person died. City directories are also a handy tool and can be found in most local libraries. All current city directories are available on the Web at www.anywho.com.

Census records are good for tracking information on a player's family. These can usually be found at genealogical libraries or at a National Records Center. They become available seventy-two years after the census (i.e., the 1930 census becomes available in 2002) and include a soundex (which assigns a numeric code to each letter), as well as the record itself.

There are several sources available on the Web. Among the most useful is the Social Security Death Index, which has the death date and residence for most people who died after 1962. This can be found at www.ancestry.com/search/rectype/vital/ssdi/main.htm. The Church of Jesus Christ of Latter-Day Saints (the Mormons) has a number of databases that are searchable on the Web. They are available to anyone who purchases a "library card" from Ancestry.com for a nominal fee. This can be done by visiting their Web site at www.ancestry.com/main.htm.

Many times it helps to get in touch with other researchers. Typically, they keep notes they made on players, which often provide information to biographical researchers. But, as with anything, there is no substitute for good, old-fashioned hard work.

70. Sowell, Mike. *The Pitch That Killed*. New York: Macmillan, 1989, 330 pp. The Cleveland Indians, New York Yankees, Ray Chapman, Carl Mays, and the 1920 pennant race.

71. Clark, Tom. *Champagne and Baloney: The Rise and Fall of Finley's A's*. New York: Harper & Row, 1976, 432 pp. The gifted poet turns his eye on the early 1970s A's championship team and its owner.

Team Histories: The Picture Book

As the relative cost of color printing has come down, these books have proliferated. Properly used, such books may provide helpful information. Many are almost entirely pictures, but some combine a large number of photos with text. For example …

72. Broeg, Bob. *Bob Broeg's Redbirds: A Century of Cardinals' Baseball*. Marceline, MO: Walsworth Publishing Co., 1992, 232 pp. This is the third edition, with the first two published in 1981 and 1987 by River City Publishing of St. Louis. A coffee-table book that combines a wide selection of pictures with Broeg's text.

BIOGRAPHIES AND AUTOBIOGRAPHIES

Depending on your subject matter, biographies and autobiographies can be highly useful. The better books will have indexes, footnotes, and bibliographies to guide you to other sources. But even the "as told to" books that form the afternoon soap operas of baseball literature can provide insight on teammates, managers, and competitors which will help you understand the subject of your research better.

There are literally thousands of biographies and autobiographies available. Here are some examples of books that are outstanding in one way or another:

73. Pietrusza, David A. *Judge and Jury: The Life and Times of Judge Kenesaw Mountain Landis*. South Bend, IN.: Diamond Communications, 1998, 564 pp. Pietrusza's book contains the kind of academic references that leave good trails for researchers following in his wake. He takes a balanced and judicious approach to the many controversies of Landis's career as commissioner.

74. Murdock, Eugene C. *Ban Johnson: Czar of Baseball*. Westport, CT: Greenwood Press, 1982, 294 pp. This is a fine, scholarly book in its own right, offering an excellent view of the organization and economics of the game at the turn of the twentieth century. But it is worth separate critical notice for the fine bibliographic essay Murdock includes.

75. Kahn, Roger. *The Boys of Summer*. New York: Harper & Row, 1972, 442 pp. This is more a primary source than a collective biography because it relies

more on the author's impressions and direct knowledge of the Brooklyn Dodgers of the early 1950s than it does on research. Superbly crafted, it is an example of the kind of writing that can be brought to baseball research.

76. Broeg, Bob. ***Superstars of Baseball***. South Bend, IN: Diamond Communications, 1994, 531 pp. This is an updated and expanded version of the 1971 edition of 329 pp. published by The Sporting News. Like Kahn's book, *Superstars of Baseball* falls somewhere between a primary source and a detached series of profiles. Having covered baseball for half a century, Broeg knew personally many of the men profiled, and he draws upon the length and depth of these relationships in creating these portraits.

77. Ritter, Lawrence S. ***The Glory of Their Times: The Story of the Early Days of Baseball Told by the Men Who Played It***. Rev. ed. New York: William Morrow, 1984, 368 pp. Ritter spawned the highly useful practice of lengthy interviews with baseball figures. The baseball world is full of these books now, and they can contribute wonderful anecdotal material to your research. Ritter, through his selection of subjects, the quality of his questioning, and the deftness of his editing, remains the model for other interviewers. This volume contains thirty interviews. The original, published by Macmillan in 1966, contained twenty-six.

78. Ritter, Lawrence S., and Mark Rucker. ***The Babe: A Life in Pictures***. New York: Ticknor & Fields, 1988, 282 pp. As with team histories, the changes in printing technology have led to more picture-oriented biographies. This book combines the formidable talents of Ritter as writer and Rucker as photo researcher.

79. Whittingham, Richard, compiler and editor. ***The DiMaggio Albums***, 2 vols. New York: G.P. Putnam's Sons, 1989, 800 pp. This is the scrapbook approach to biography. The two volumes are a compilation of facsimiles of newspaper articles, pictures, cartoons, and box scores, with little connecting material supplied by the editor.

Autobiographies are often less useful than books done by more objective chroniclers. But skillful questioning and thoughtful editing can turn an interview-based book into a flowing narrative. A couple of good examples are...

80. Veeck, Bill, and Ed Linn. ***Veeck—As in Wreck***. New York: G.P. Putnam's Sons, 1962, 380 pp.

81. Robinson, Jackie, and Alfred Duckett. ***I Never Had It Made***. New York: G.P. Putnam's Sons, 1972, 287 pp.

FICTION AND POETRY

Fiction is not a historical research source, although the novels of Eric Rolfe Greenberg (*The Celebrant*), Darryl Brock (*If I Never Get Back*), Luke Salisbury (*The Cleveland Indian*), and Troy Soos (*Murder at Fenway Park* and several other mysteries starring fictitious utility infielder/detective Mickey Rawlings) show strong research by the authors.

Novels can be useful sources for reflecting a player's image in the broader populace. Many players, either explicitly or under obvious pseudonyms, appear in novels such as *The Celebrant*, which deals extensively with a player's image as hero (in this case Christy Mathewson) and what that means to fans and players.

Several players, beginning in 1910 with Frank Chance's *The Bride and the Pennant* and Christy Mathewson's *Won in the Ninth* have had novels published under their names, indicating the pull of that player for marketing purposes, if not their literary talent.

Although poets such as Walt Whitman and Marianne Moore have waxed poetic about baseball, the only subject of serious baseball poetry research has been *Casey at the Bat*. See Eugene Murdock's *Mighty Casey: All-American*. Westport, CT: Greenwood Press, 1984, 164 pp., for the ultimate discussion of the poem. See Martin Gardner's *The Annotated Casey at the Bat: A Collection of Ballads About the Mighty Casey*. New York: Clarkson N. Potter, 1967, 206 pp., for some wonderful, less-than-serious research on the poem.

BOOKS ON SPECIAL TOPICS

These topics are chosen from a much larger host of possibilities, mostly because they reflect SABR's committee structure and, therefore, presumably its research interests. In many cases, the relevant committee has played an active role in fostering the research, or bringing people together, or providing raw materials to authors.

Through some of the works mentioned below, SABR committees have started to create a research infrastructure, books that future researchers can turn to in answering basic questions about a field. In each area, any such infrastructure works are mentioned along with books that represent the possibilities for research sources. These lists are by no means exhaustive and many fine works have been left out. And, because many of the encyclopedias, guides, and registers, which make up the infrastructure are first editions, revisions and updates are still being made.

Minor Leagues

82. Johnson, Lloyd, and Miles Wolff, eds. ***The Encyclopedia of Minor League Baseball, Second edition***. Durham, NC: Baseball America, 1997, 666 pp. This volume lists such information as the years that each league existed, the years in which cities had teams, the standings, managers, and attendance for each team by year, as well as other basic material. A constant reference source for minor league researchers, it contains a very useful bibliography.

83. Bauer, Carlos, ed. *The SABR Guide to Minor League Statistics*. Cleveland: The Society for American Baseball Research, 1995, 158 pp. From year to year, the guides tended to change which minor leagues' statistics they reported and what categories. This guide allows you to start with either a league and year or a guide and find out whether any minor league statistics are available and if so, which ones.

84. *Minor League Baseball Research Journal*. Cleveland: Society for American Baseball Research, 1991-1997. Originally known as the *Minor League History Journal*, for three issues, and then this title for two more, the *Journal* produced some groundbreaking work in minor league research.

85. Finch, Robert L., L.H. Addington, and Ben P. Morgan. *The Story of Minor League Baseball*. Columbus, OH: The National Association of Professional Baseball Leagues, 1953, 744 pp. The official history of the minors, written at a time when television's near fatal inroads had barely begun to be visible.

86. Sullivan, Neil. *The Minors: The Struggles and the Triumph of Baseball's Poor Relation from 1876 to the Present*. New York: St. Martin's Press, 1990, 307 pp. This book presents little original historical research, but it is probably the finest analytical history of the minor leagues and their relationship with the majors. Very useful in understanding the context in which a league or team had to live.

The number of minor league histories has been proliferating. Here are some examples:

87. O'Neal, Bill. *The Texas League, 1888-1987: A Century of Baseball*. Austin, TX: Eakin Press, 1987, 389 pp. O'Neal and Eakin Press have also published histories of the American Association (1991), the International League (1992), the Pacific Coast League (1990) and the Southern League (1994). All are workmanlike efforts.

88. Chrisman, David F. *A History of the Piedmont League*. Self-published, 1986, 226 pp. Chrisman's work is a good example of a dedicated fan-researcher publishing the fruits of his work. Chrisman also published a three-volume history of the International League in the early 1980s.

89. Zingg, Paul J., and Mark D. Medeiros. *Runs, Hits and an Era: The Pacific Coast League, 1903-1958*. Urbana, IL: University of Illinois Press, 1994, 170 pp. Outstanding illustrations, team statistics, and footnotes make this well-researched book exceptionally useful.

Researchers have also begun to turn out statistical histories of various minor leagues, which can supplement and correct the material in the guides. Three examples are...

90. Wright, Marshall D. *The American Association: Year-by-Year Statistics for the Baseball Minor League, 1902-1952*. Jefferson, NC: McFarland & Co., 1997, 408pp.

91. Wright, Marshall D. *The International League: Year-by-Year Statistics, 1884-1953*. Jefferson, NC: McFarland & Co., 1998, 538 pp.

92. Snelling, Dennis. *The Pacific Coast League: A Statistical History, 1903-1957*. Jefferson, NC: McFarland & Co., 1995, 392 pp.

Individual teams, or cities, are also a growing area for researchers. Some examples:

93. Beverage, Richard E. *The Hollywood Stars: Baseball in Movieland, 1926-1957*. Placentia, CA: Deacon Press, 1984, 311 pp.

94. Beverage, Richard E. *The Angels: Los Angeles in the Pacific Coast League, 1919-1957*. Placentia, CA: Deacon Press, 1981, 286 pp. Beverage's two team histories from the old Pacific Coast League contain useful appendices on rosters, statistics, and uniform numbers.

95. Mayer, Ronald A. *The 1937 Newark Bears: A Baseball Legend*. Rev. ed. New Brunswick, NJ: Rutgers University Press, 1994, 300 pp. History that emphasizes a single season. Mayer argues that the '37 Bears team was the greatest minor league aggregation of all time.

96. McCombs, Wayne. *"Let's Go Tulsa!": The History of Professional Baseball in Tulsa, Oklahoma, 1905-1989*. Self-published, 1990, 537 pp. This follows the history of minor league baseball in a single city, through several leagues, ownership groups, and major league affiliations.

97. Panek, Richard. *Waterloo Diamonds*. New York: St. Martin's Press, 1995, 373 pp. Considerably more focused on off-the-field relationships than most minor league histories, it is not so much a history as a look at the modern situation.

98. Spalding, John E. *Sacramento Senators and Solons: Baseball in California's Capital, 1886 to 1976*. San Jose, CA: John E. Spalding, 1995, 200 pp. A franchise history with a little more than usual in the way of pictures and a close eye on the financial roller coaster of keeping the team alive.

SABR's venerable *Minor League Baseball Stars* remains a useful resource for researchers tracking individual careers. The three volumes, all edited by L. Robert Davids, appeared in 1978 (125 pp.), 1985 (158 pp.), and 1992 (184 pp.). They contain career records for over 600 players. These three volumes were subsumed into...

99. Johnson, Lloyd, ed. *The Minor League Register*. Durham, NC: Baseball America, 1994, 480 pp. This book extends the research and covers 870 players.

Negro Leagues

The Negro Leagues have been the subject of some of the most intensive baseball research of the past two decades. While much remains to be done, the framework for this study has been established.

100. Clark, Dick, and Larry Lester, eds. *The Negro Leagues Book*. Cleveland: Society for American Baseball Research, 1994, 382 pp. The basic reference book, it covers rosters, standings, records, the East-West game, and players who moved from the Negro Leagues to the white leagues. It also contains a good, short history of the Negro Leagues and profiles of Negro Leaguers in the Hall of Fame. A very useful bibliography is included.

101. Riley, James A. *The Biographical Encyclopedia of the Negro Baseball Leagues*. New York: Carroll & Graf Publishers, 1994, 926 pp. This volume covers over 4,000 players who performed in African-American baseball from 1872 through the 1950s. A full entry—and many entries are less than full because of a lack of information—includes name, years, position, teams in both the Negro Leagues and the white leagues, bats-throws, height, weight, and birth date and place. There is also an essay on the player's career. Each team receives a listing. There is a good bibliography at the end.

102. Peterson, Robert. *Only the Ball Was White*. Englewood Cliffs, NJ: Prentice-Hall, 1970, 406 pp. The first full-length history of the Negro Leagues, still a basic source and the starting point for many of the current researchers.

103. Dixon, Phil, with Patrick J. Hannigan. *The Negro Baseball Leagues: A Photographic History*. Mattituck, NY: Amereon House, 1992, 364 pp. An unparalleled photographic record of the Negro Leagues.

104. Tygiel, Jules. *Baseball's Great Experiment: Jackie Robinson and His Legacy*. New York: Oxford University Press, 1997, 413 pp. An expanded and updated version of the 1983 original. While often thought of as a biography of Robinson, it is actually a look at the whole process of integrating the game (and destroying the Negro Leagues in the process).

Team histories from the Negro Leagues are relatively sparse. Four worthwhile ones are:

105. Bankes, James. *The Pittsburgh Crawfords: The Lives & Times of Baseball's Most Exciting Team*. Dubuque, IA: William C. Brown, 1991, 173 pp.

106. Bruce, Janet. *The Kansas City Monarchs: Champions of Black Baseball*. Lawrence, KS: University Press of Kansas, 1985, 176 pp.

107. DeBono, Paul. *The Indianapolis ABC's: The History of a Premier Team in the Negro Leagues*. Jefferson, NC: McFarland & Co., 1997, 231 pp.

108. Lanctot, Neil. *Fair Dealing and Clean Playing: The Hilldale Club and the Development of Black Professional Baseball, 1910-1932*. Jefferson, NC: McFarland & Co., 1994, 298 pp.

Biographies of Negro League players are becoming much more common...

109. Brashler, William. *Josh Gibson: A Life in the Negro Leagues*. New York: Harper & Row, 1978, 193 pp. The best life story of the enigmatic slugger.

110. Overmyer, James. *Queen of the Negro Leagues: Effa Manley and the Newark Eagles*. Lanham, MD: The Scarecrow Press, 1998, 297 pp. Follows the career of one of the few female owners in professional baseball and explores the issue of how the majors stripped black teams of their young stars and thus destroyed the Negro Leagues. Issued in 1993 as *Effa Manley and the Newark Eagles*.

111. Leonard, Buck, with James A. Riley. *Buck Leonard: The Black Lou Gehrig, the Hall of Famer's Story in His Own Words*. New York: Carroll & Graf, 1995, 286 pp. One of the more successful of the as-told-to genre, especially as few Negro Leagues stars have the multiple biographies of white stars.

112. Robinson, Frazier "Slow," with Paul Bauer. *Catching Dreams: My Life in the Negro Baseball Leagues*. Syracuse, NY: Syracuse University Press, 1999, 230 pp. Another successful as-told-to, with two additional elements. Robinson was a successful journeyman, not a star, and we have rarely seen this angle on the Negro Leagues. In addition, he did a great deal of catching for Satchel Paige and provides new material on the Hall of Famer.

113. Bak, Richard. *Turkey Stearnes and the Detroit Stars: The Negro Leagues in Detroit, 1919-1933*. Detroit: Wayne State University Press, 1994, 298 pp. More than a biography of the slugging outfielder, this book looks at the African-American community in Detroit and its place in the larger city.

114. Holway, John B. *Voices from the Great Black Baseball Leagues*, Rev. ed. New York: Da Capo Press, 1992, 403 pp. A collection of oral histories, this edition includes additional material, mostly pictures and statistics. The original was published by Dodd, Mead & Co. in 1975.

Ballparks

In addition to the next three books, the Ballparks Committee maintains files containing articles, papers, and other research material on ballparks and stadium-related issues. Contact the Ballparks Committee chair as listed in the most recent *SABR Membership Directory*. For a more definitive look at stadium books, see John Pastier, "Baseball Loci: A Survey of Ballpark Books." *Elysian Fields Quarterly*, World Series Issue, 1992.

115. Benson, Michael. ***Ballparks of North America: A Comprehensive Historical Reference to Baseball Grounds, Yards and Stadiums, 1845 to Present***. Jefferson, NC: McFarland & Co., 1989, 475 pp. Organized by cities, this remains the most comprehensive source on ballparks in existence, although it has certain errors and omissions. Also includes many minor league parks. Further research is producing more information on dimensions, modifications, and other issues, but this is still the best place to start.

116. Lowry, Philip J. ***Green Cathedrals: The Ultimate Celebration of All 271 Major League and Negro League Ballparks Past and Present***. Reading, MA: Addison-Wesley Publishing Co., 1992, 275 pp. This is an expanded and updated version of the book published by SABR in 1986. It is also organized by cities and contains many pictures. The SABR version was pockmarked with errors, poorly organized, and yet clearly the best thing published on ballparks up to that time. The Addison-Wesley edition clears up a good many of the errors and includes more photographs than were in the original. The cost of the illustrations is a severe reduction in the amount of text.

In recent years, as several classic ballparks were torn down or threatened, books about them have proliferated. While some of these books are quite good reading, they often tend to be chronicles of what happened in the ballparks rather than of the parks themselves— more team history than stadium history. Tiger Stadium and Fenway Park have been the recipients of several such treatments. While the text of these books is often of limited use in stadium research, the books are usually extensively illustrated, and the pictures can prove valuable.

117. Richmond, Peter. ***Ballpark: Camden Yards and the Building of an American Dream***. New York: Simon & Schuster, 1993, 284 pp. This is an exception to the broad statement above, as this book focuses on the politics and design considerations that went into the stadium nobody calls "Oriole Park at Camden Yards," its official name.

Umpires

Material about umpires in book form is, unfortunately, scanty and highly anecdotal. We still lack, for example, full rosters of umpires for many major league seasons, although the Umpire and Rules Committee is working steadily to complete them. The committee also maintains an archive of research materials.

118. Kahn, James M. ***The Umpire Story***. New York: G.P. Putnam's Sons, 1953, 247 pp. Produced as part of the Putnam's baseball series that centered around team histories. A very anecdotal book which pulls together a lot of the famous stories about umpires.

119. Skipper, John C. *Umpires: Classic Baseball Stories from the Men Who Made the Calls*. Jefferson, NC: McFarland & Co., 1997, 180 pp. Oral histories and anecdotes.

120. Gerlach, Larry. *Men in Blue: Conversations with Umpires*. New York: Viking, 1980, 287 pp. Reissued by University of Nebraska Press in 1994. In-depth conversations with a dozen umpires who worked many decades. Includes an interview with Ernie Stewart, blackballed for his involvement in forming an umpires' union.

There are not many umpire biographies. Here are a few:

121. Johnson, Steamboat. *Standing the Gaff*. Nashville, TN: Parthenon Press, 1935, 142 pp. Reissued by University of Nebraska Press in 1994 with new introduction. The earliest umpire biography, written by a long-time umpire in the Southern Association.

122. Gorman, Tom, as told to Jerome Holtzman. *Three and Two!* New York: Charles Scribner's Sons, 1979, 216 pp. Probably the most realistic of the autobiographies.

123. Gutkind, Lee. *The Best Seat in Baseball, but You Have to Stand*. New York: The Dial Press, 1975, 209 pp. Gutkind followed Doug Harvey's crew for a year and then wrote this book. The crew members hated it.

The Business of Baseball

With all the off-the-field problems of baseball in recent years, the economic and legal side of the game has become the topic for considerable research. Many of the best books wrap baseball in with other professional sports, but their conclusions about the game are still valuable, even if you do have to read about hockey to get there.

124. **Celler Hearings**. In 1952, 1957, 1958 and 1960, the House Committee on the Judiciary Antitrust Subcommittee under chairman Emanuel Celler held hearings on sports. While the material is most famous for the exchange in which Mickey Mantle says he agrees completely with the several minutes of doubletalk just spouted by Casey Stengel, the first two sets of hearings contain unprecedented information on profits and costs of major league operations in the first half of the century. There is also extensive material on the reserve clause and on baseball's relationship with television. Later hearings, especially the last, dealt heavily with other sports. These publications can

usually be found only at libraries that set themselves up as depositories of congressional publications. They are formally known as *Organized Professional Team Sports: Hearings before the Antitrust Subcommittee (Subcommittee No. 5) of the Committee on the Judiciary, House of Representatives*.

125. Burk, Robert F. *Never Just a Game: Players, Owners, and American Baseball to 1920*. Chapel Hill, NC: The University of North Carolina Press, 1994, 284 pp. A well-researched book, which, if nothing else, serves as a reminder that baseball's economic warfare did not begin in recent decades.

126. Lowenfish, Lee, and Tony Lupien. *The Imperfect Diamond: The Story of Baseball's Reserve System and the Men Who Fought to Change It*. New York: Stein and Day, 1980, 258 pp. Focusing on the reserve clause, this book was written with a former player's personal knowledge and with the destruction of the reserve clause in the recent past.

127. Helyar, John. *Lords of the Realm: The Real History of Baseball*. New York: Villard Books, 1994, 576 pp. Probably the best overall history of baseball's labor troubles, although focused on the decades since the appearance of Marvin Miller. Written by a *Wall Street Journal* reporter, it is much more readable than the work of many of the economists.

128. Noll, Roger G., ed. *Government and the Sports Business*. Washington, DC: The Brookings Institution, 1974, 445 pp. Noll was an economist who consulted with the Players Union on economic issues.

Although Noll's collection touches on what would become many of the major themes for future economists, its emphasis is on the role of government agencies in dealing with sports teams.

129. Scully, Gerard W. *The Business of Major League Baseball*. Chicago: University of Chicago Press, 1989, 212 pp. Scully analyzes, from an economist's viewpoint, issues of stadiums, media revenues, competition, salaries, and other matters bedeviling the sport.

130. Quirk, James, and Rodney Fort. *Pay Dirt: The Business of Professional Team Sports*. Princeton, NJ: Princeton University Press, 1992, 538 pp.

131. Quirk, James, and Rodney Fort. *Hard Ball: The Abuse of Power in Team Sports*. Princeton, NJ: Princeton University Press, 1999, 233 pp.

Quirk's two-book collection addresses many of the same issues as Scully's book, but with fresher data. Unlike Scully, the contributors wander over the entire sports world.

132. Miller, Marvin. *A Whole Different Ball Game: The Sport and Business of Baseball*. New York: Birch Lane Press, 1991, 430 pp. Nominally an autobiography, this is a complement to Helyar's work (#127). Well worth studying since Miller was the most powerful figure in the sport for two decades.

133. Abrams, Roger I. *Legal Bases: Baseball and the Law*. Philadelphia: Temple University Press, 1998, 226 pp. Focuses on the important legal issues of baseball, from the reserve clause to the Pete Rose suspension, by telling stories built around six players, two owners, a union leader, and a federal judge.

NINETEENTH-CENTURY BASEBALL

This is another area that has benefited from extensive published research in the last decade. Reference should also be made to the first volume of Seymour's work (#50) and of Sullivan's document collections (#54) in the General History section above.

134. Nemec, David. *The Great Encyclopedia of 19th-Century Major League Baseball*. New York: Donald I. Fine Books, 1997, 852 pp. This is mainly a statistical work, but it includes significant text material, including year-by-year summaries. Nemec includes fielding statistics, umpire rosters, and much other hard-to-find material. An indispensable starting point for nineteenth-century research, especially because it has a good bibliography.

135. Tiemann, Robert L., and Mark Rucker, eds. *Nineteenth Century Stars*. Kansas City, MO: Society for American Baseball Research, 1989, 144 pp.

136. Ivor-Campbell, Fred, Robert L. Tiemann, and Mark Rucker, eds. *Baseball's First Stars*. Cleveland: Society for American Baseball Research, 1996, 183 pp. Together, these books profile 289 players, owners, organizers, umpires, and other figures from the nineteenth century.

137. Leitner, Irving A. *Baseball: Diamond in the Rough*. New York: Criterion Books, 1972, 226 pp. A fine, well-written general introduction to baseball and its early years.

The three histories listed below chronicle three important periods in the nineteenth century—the period of growing organization and professionalization, the first professional league, and the first economic and athletic competition between professional leagues:

138. Ryczek, William J. *When Johnny Came Sliding Home: The Post-Civil War Baseball Boom, 1865-1870*. Jefferson, NC: McFarland & Co., 1998, 313 pp.

139. Ryczek, William J. *Blackguards and Red Stockings: A History of Baseball's National Association, 1871-1875*. Jefferson, NC: McFarland & Co., 1992, 272 pp.

by John R. Husman / Nineteenth Century Committee

More than a third of baseball's recorded history happened during the nineteenth century. Throughout the mid and late 1800s the volume of baseball's written record increased exponentially. Well before the end of the century, guides were regularly published, sporting newspapers were available, and histories had begun to be written. Primary research sources and methods described in Chapter 3 and elsewhere in this book readily apply. But the earliest history of the game, the period from 1845 (and even before) to the advent of the professional era in 1871, provides a special challenge to the person doing research—lack of sources.

As always, the most available primary source is the newspaper. However, the meager baseball-related content that newspapers included during these early years was commingled with other news, making its retrieval extremely tedious. Additionally, this early baseball news was very much localized. There are no easy, one-source answers to questions about early baseball in, say, Philadelphia, or Binghamton, or Grand Rapids. The solution is to spend hours at the microfilm reader, searching through the pages of local newspapers.

Other primary sources for these early years include club records and scoring books. These may be found at local historical societies or local history sections of public libraries and university libraries. Don't expect to find a large quantity of material, but some early clubs did keep complete and meticulous records.

Descendents of early baseball people may have primary-source information about their ancestor. This information can include diaries, letters, photographs, scrapbooks, and perhaps even personal memorabilia. Often these descendents are pleased that their ball-playing forebear is being recognized, and are quite willing to share information about him. Finding such a person, however, is always time-consuming and can be difficult. The search might be called "reverse genealogy," because to find a living descendent you must work forward in time, generation by generation. Starting with the ballplayer in question, you have to identify his children (males are much easier to trace), and then their children. Some good sources of information are newspaper obituary notices, city directories, and the United States census. Church records may be difficult to find, but can be virtual gold mines if you do. As you work through generations to recent years, you may find telephone directories useful, especially for uncommon names. Even common names can sometimes be traced. The family of New York Knickerbocker "Dock" Adams, for instance, was found in a Buffalo telephone directory.

Researching the early years of baseball, and joining in the pursuit of finding earlier and earlier roots of our national game, is a challenge, to be sure. The sources are limited, but the rewards are great.

140. Nemec, David, with Mark Rucker, picture ed. *The Beer and Whisky League: The Illustrated History of the American Association—Baseball's Renegade Major League*. New York: Lyons & Burford, 1994, 260 pp.

The following three books place the game, its origins, and organization in a broad cultural and economic context:

141. Adelman, Melvin L. *A Sporting Time: New York City and the Rise of Modern Athletics*. Urbana, IL: University of Illinois Press, 1986, 388 pp.
142. Goldstein, Warren. *Playing for Keeps: A History of Early Baseball*. Ithaca, NY: Cornell University Press, 1989, 182 pp.
143. Kirsch, George B. *The Creation of American Team Sports*. Urbana, IL: University of Illinois Press, 1989, 277 pp.
144. Levine, Peter. *A.G. Spalding and the Rise of Baseball: The Promise of American Sport*. New York: Oxford University Press, 1985, 184 pp. Portrays the rise of the sport through the career of a man who went from player to official to manufacturer, cashing in on the sport's popularity.
145. DiSalvatore, Bryan. *A Clever Base-Ballist: The Life and Times of John Montgomery Ward*. New York: Pantheon, 1999, 477 pp. A bit overwritten, but a useful chronicle of one of the century's most interesting figures. As player, manager, and official, most notably in his attempts to form the Players League in 1890, Ward participated in many of the key baseball events of the century.
146. Hetrick, J. Thomas. *Chris Von der Ahe and the St. Louis Browns*. Lanham, MD: The Scarecrow Press, 1999, 284 pp. Traces the rise and fall of Von der Ahe, one of the first magnates to successfully use baseball to promote his other businesses.

WOMEN

147. Berlage, Gai Ingham. *Women in Baseball: The Forgotten History*. Westport, CT: Praeger Publishers, 1994, 208 pp.
148. Gregorich, Barbara. *Women at Play: The Story of Women in Baseball*. San Diego: Harcourt, Brace & Co., 1993, 214 pp. These are the two basic histories of women's role in the game.
149. Johnson, Susan E. *When Women Played Hardball*. Seattle: Seal Press, 1994, 292 pp. A history of the All-American Girls Professional Baseball League.
150. Madden, W.C. *The Women of the All-American Girls Professional Baseball League*. Jefferson, NC: McFarland & Co., 1997, 288 pp. Statistical summaries and short profiles of the AAGPBL's players. Lots of pictures.

INTERNATIONAL BASEBALL

The best source on international baseball generally is *The National Pastime* of 1992 (dubbed *The International Pastime* for that issue), edited by Peter C. Bjarkman and containing a wide range of articles from the Olympics to baseball in various countries. There is also a bimonthly magazine called *International Baseball* (see members.aol.com/ibrundown). Otherwise, most writing and research on the topic has been devoted to individual countries or regions. The suggestions below cover only books published in English. A wealth of material awaits the researcher capable of reading Spanish, Japanese, or any other language in which baseball writing appears.

Latin America in General

151. Bjarkman, Peter C. *Baseball with a Latin Beat*. Jefferson, NC: McFarland & Co., 1994, 460 pp. An overview of baseball as played throughout the Caribbean basin and the mainland of South and Central America.

Cuba

152. Gonzalez Echevarria, Roberto. *The Pride of Havana: A History of Cuban Baseball*. New York: Oxford University Press, 1999, 464 pp.

Dominican Republic

153. Ruck, Rob. *The Tropic of Baseball: Baseball in the Dominican Republic*. Westport, CT: Meckler Books, 1991, 205 pp.

154. Joyce, Gare. *The Only Ticket Off the Island*. Toronto: Lester & Orpen Dennys, Publishers, 1990, 229 pp.

Puerto Rico

155. Van Hyning, Thomas E. *Puerto Rico's Winter League: A History of Major League Baseball's Launching Pad*. Jefferson, NC: McFarland & Co., 1995, 290 pp.

Japan

There are a few good books on Japanese baseball in English, but most deal with Americans in Japan and are written from the American point of view.

156. Graczyk, Wayne, comp. and ed. *Japan Pro Baseball Fan Handbook and Media Guide*. Durham, NC: Baseball America, 1988-present. Basic facts and figures. Little history, with an emphasis on the American presence.

157. Obojski, Robert. *The Rise of Japanese Baseball Power*. Radnor, PA: Chilton Book Co., 1975, 230 pp. Stiffly written and getting outdated, but the best overall history of Japanese baseball in English.

158. Whiting, Robert C. The *Chrysanthemum and the Bat*. New York: Dodd, Mead & Co., 1977, 247 pp.

159. Whiting, Robert C. *You Gotta Have Wa*. New York: Macmillan, 1989, 339 pp. Two wonderfully written books that focus on the differences between American and Japanese baseball and the problems of American players who have gone to Japan.

160. Oh, Sadaharu, with David Falkner. *Sadaharu Oh: A Zen Way of Baseball*. New York: Times Books, 1984, 279 pp. An as-told-to biography which provides more insight than usual into the game from the Japanese point of view.

Canada

161. Humber, William. *Diamonds of the North: A Concise History of Baseball in Canada*. Toronto: Oxford University Press, 1995, 238 pp.

162. Shearon, Jim. *Canada's Baseball Legends*. Kanata, Ontario: Malin Head Press, 1994, 248 pp. Profiles of Canadian-born major leaguers.

163. Hack, Paul, and Dave Shury. *Wheat Province Diamonds: A Story of Saskatchewan Baseball*. Regina, Saskatchewan: Saskatchewan Baseball Association, Inc., 1997, 404 pp. This is one example of a growing trend for regional histories of baseball in various Canadian provinces and regions.

UNPUBLISHED SOURCES

Not everything has been published in book form or entered on the Internet.

There is nothing quite like the SABR Research Exchange, run by Len Levin (282 Doyle Ave., Providence, RI 02906). Levin compiles presentations at SABR regionals and the national convention, short research pieces by SABR members, photocopies of articles from a variety of publications, and other materials. A list of the available material can be obtained for $3. There is a charge for photocopying.

University Microfilms International (now known as UMI and owned by Bell & Howell) covers masters' theses and doctoral dissertations since 1861. Copies of many papers are available for roughly $25. The address is Bell & Howell Information and Learning, 300 North Zeeb Road, P.O. Box 1346, Ann Arbor, MI 48106-1346.

On the Internet, see www.umi.com/hp/Products/Dissertations.html.

WHERE TO FIND THEM

Many of the books cited here, and others you may decide you need for your research, are out of print. Here is a short list of used book dealers who specialize in baseball books. All are SABR members and all deal through the mail.

- Paul Bauer, Archer's Used and Rare Books
  104 S. Lincoln St., Kent, OH 44240. Phone: (330) 673-0945

- Wayne Greene
  945 West End Ave., #5D, New York, NY 10025. Phone: (212) 662-2104.

- Richard Miller
  8010 Nob Hill Dr., Ft. Thomas, KY 41075-1493. Phone: (606) 441-8646.

- R."Bobby" Plapinger
  P.O. Box 1062, Ashland, OR 97520. Phone: (541) 488-1220.

You might also find it useful to go to an Internet search site for used books, such as www.bookfinder.com, which taps into book dealers around the world and is searchable by author, title, and subject.

Chapter Four
USING THE COMPUTER
FOR BASEBALL RESEARCH
by Jed Hathaway

The advent of electronic data storage and transmission in general, and the Internet in particular, has brought many new capabilities and opportunities for the baseball researcher. The largest factor in this change is the nature of the resources we use. But the new technologies have also affected how we retrieve and transmit information, contact individuals and organizations, even the way we write and present our research.

While it is just as possible as ever to do excellent research using relatively few electronic resources, it is no longer possible to ignore them completely. In any event, researchers who hope to disregard the new technologies are simply shortchanging themselves. The way we gather, store, and transmit information is undergoing a gradual evolution from a predominantly paper-based medium to an electronic-based one. This new electronic universe may sometimes be daunting, but it presents tools and methods impossible to employ using traditional paper resources. The world has never ceased changing and researchers must learn to adapt and realize that change is sometimes for the better.

This chapter will cover many electronic resources and describe some useful techniques for locating information using the new technologies. Given the constantly changing nature of the Web, it is just as important to know how to locate information and information resources as it is to be aware of what sources are currently available.

EQUIPMENT: Computers

An important but not necessarily vital step in using computers for your research is obtaining a computer and computer software of your own. This need not be an expensive or complicated undertaking. Powerful, up-to-date equipment and program packages are readily available for little more than $500. Used equipment, which is more than adequate for most research needs, can be had for as little as $100. A great deal of information is available to the consumer on the many different kinds of equipment and software. There is not enough space to discuss and evaluate them here. Instead, this chapter will cover the basic computing tools and how the researcher can use them.

Software

The most common computer program, and the easiest to use, is the word processing program. This is what you use to organize your data, write your drafts, prepare columns, tables, or other graphic information, and put your research into final form for printing. Essentially, it is your typing program.

A word processing program offers a variety of features to help the writer:

- ❶ easy copying, moving, inserting, and editing of text;
- ❶ changing the size and appearance of the text in many different ways;
- ❶ easy creation or adding of charts, graphs, tables, images, and columns, and
- ❶ basic spelling and grammatical proofreading functions.

Some common word processing programs are Microsoft Word, Word Perfect, or the word processing programs that are part of the Microsoft Works and Apple Works suites.

Other standard software tools include spreadsheets and database programs. Spreadsheets are invaluable for organizing and manipulating statistical data. Database programs are great for gathering and organizing data that you can later search, sort, and present in many ways. Some examples of these types of programs are Lotus 1-2-3, Microsoft Excel, Microsoft Access, Paradox, and FileMaker Pro.

However, the researcher who uses only a word processing program can do much. While it is helpful to understand the many possibilities offered by software programs for the home computer, you are not obliged to buy them all. Nor should you feel it necessary to learn about every aspect of a given program before using it. As with any tool, it pays to know what you need it for in the first place before you purchase it.

Email

Email is a useful tool for the researcher. With it, you can communicate quickly and inexpensively with organizations, other researchers, editors, publishers—anyone with an email address. You can send written messages, documents, programs, images, or other computer files to one or many individuals or organizations.

You can also subscribe to online discussion or exchange groups, such as SABR-L. This is an Internet listserv, or bulletin board, available only to SABR members. SABR-L is an important information resource for members seeking information on any baseball research project. More information on SABR-L can be found at the SABR Web site (www.sabr.org).

Basic email service is usually quite inexpensive. In fact, if you have an Internet connection, providers like Yahoo (www.yahoo.com), Hotmail (www.hotmail.com), or Netscape WebMail (www.netscape.com), offer free email.

Please note: Web site addresses sometimes change. The addresses listed in this chapter were current in early 2000. They may no longer be valid when you read this.

The Internet

The Internet is a vast communications domain consisting of millions of Web sites, email addresses, and other functions residing on computers interlinked through telecommunications networks. It is also a medium that lets researchers access sources of information on all subjects. While the claim that "you can find out everything about anything on the Internet" is hogwash, the significance of the Internet as an information resource should not be underestimated.

Accessing the Internet/WWW (World Wide Web) may be free—as through a local library. Typically, full access costs about $20 a month. Internet service providers ("ISPs") are listed in your local yellow pages.

Communications or Email Programs

Email is typically accessed using a communications program, such as Pegasus, Eudora, Microsoft Outlook, or Netscape Communicator. Such programs allow you to connect with your email service provider and to send and receive email messages, including attached files. Communications programs are available inexpensively through local computer stores and media outlets. Many programs are also available for free over the Internet. For example: Pegasus (www.pegasus.com) or Eudora (www.eudora.com). Obtaining these free programs involves what is called "downloading." From many Web sites, it is possible to copy computer files and programs directly to your home computer. Depending on the speed of your modem, the size of the file or program being copied, and the level of "traffic" on the Web, this process may be fairly fast or very slow.

Web Browsers

Like email, the World Wide Web is typically accessed using a communications program, although actually viewing the Web is accomplished by using an Internet browser, such as Microsoft Explorer or Netscape Navigator. Web pages are specially formatted using a system of code called HTML (Hypertext Markup Language) inserted into the text of the Web site. These determine the appearance of the text on the browser, as well as the display images and other graphics, the play sounds, and the execute programs. Browser programs are available for free over the Internet. As noted above, two familiar browsers are Microsoft Explorer (www.microsoft.com) and Netscape Navigator (www.netscape.com).

THE INTERNET: Web Sites or "Home Pages"

Web site (which is a more accurate term than "home page") refers to those strings of letters (and sometimes numbers) that have been popping up everywhere over the past few years, usually beginning with "www" and often ending with "dot com." These are locations on the World Wide Web, representing anything from a single text document to an elaborate assemblage of words, images, and sounds interlinked with dozens, hundreds, or even thousands of other Web sites. It is because of this crisscrossed interlinking (hyperlinks is the descriptive term) that the setup is called the Web. It is "world wide" because it uses our existing telecommunications networks, which are global. The World Wide Web is a great platform for words, images, and sounds that can be accessed almost instantaneously by people all over the world at low cost. Given this, it is easy to see what people are so excited about.

A word about "dot com," which almost overnight has become a household term: The *.com* (the "dot" is simply a period) indicates a commercial or an individual's site; *.org* indicates a nonprofit site; *.edu* indicates an educational institution; *.gov* indicates a government site; *.net* indicates an Internet service provider. There are also a host of country codes; for example, *.ca* for Canada; *.de* for Germany; *.au* for Australia, and so on.

Search Engines

Search engines are usually free Internet services available for searching the Web. Some common examples are the following:

- **Northern Light** (www.northernlight.com): Currently up to 190 million Web sites indexed. Generally has a lower number of dead sites than other search engines and offers many powerful search features. Includes a "special collection" service with access to full-text articles from over 3,400 sources (fee-based).
- **Alta Vista** (www.av.com): Claims to fully index more than 175 million Web sites. Also offers advanced search capabilities for more sophisticated searching, including the ability to include or exclude search terms. Online help is very useful. A good choice for comprehensive Web searches.
- **Fast** (www.alltheweb.com): Not many features, but large (200 million sites) and somewhat quicker than the others listed here.
- **Excite** (www.excite.com): Not as large as the others, but growing rapidly. Has the smallest number of "dead links" among the larger search engines.
- **Yahoo** (www.yahoo.com): A subject-oriented directory referencing thousands of sites. Includes a conventional Internet search engine (Inktomi).

Using these services, you can search millions of Web sites for information on any topic (see "Searching Tips"). It is generally a good idea to try your search using more than one search engine. Your search results will often vary. Search-engines expert Greg Notess has demonstrated that there is little overlap among different search engines in their search results. Readers should check Notess's Web site (www.notess.com) for more information on the many kinds of search engines available. With few exceptions (Northern Light is one), search engines offer little or no subject access or indexed approaches to information. The searching method or "algorithm" of most search engines is relevancy-based. This usually means taking a count of the number of times a term occurs in a given site as a means for determining relevance to the requested term. Put simply, it is a scattershot approach. Given the 100 to 200 million Web sites typically covered by most search engines, you may end up with a lot of garbage in your search results.

Multiple search engines search the Web using several search engines at the same time. Some examples of these are **Cyber411** (www.cyber411.com), **Dogpile** (www.dogpile.com) and **Metacrawler** (www.metacrawler.com). Beware of the limitations of these services. They often display only the top ten to fifty Web sites found by each search engine. They don't usually search using the advanced capabilities of each search engine. And some major search engines (e.g. Northern Light) aren't searchable using multiple search engines.

It also is important to understand the inherent limitations of search engines. They cannot search for many different kinds of documents, even though these documents may be "on the Web." For example, many government documents and statistics will not show up in search engine searches. Nor will formatted text; .pdf or image file documents; data within databases; data within framed pages; dynamic pages, or any data accessible only by subscription. Many of these resources, which constitute the so-called "Invisible Web," can be found through using specialty directories.

- **Direct Search - Price's List of Lists** (gwis2.circ.gwu.edu/~gprice/direct.htm): A growing compilation of links to the search interfaces of resources that contain data not easily or entirely searchable/accessible from general search engines like Alta Vista.
- **Lycos's "Invisible Web"** (invisibleWeb.com): Quick and advanced search functions for searching the "Invisible Web."
- **Scout Report** (wwwscout.cs.wisc.edu/): Focuses on a small but select number of in-depth resources.
- **Librarian's Index to the Internet** (sunsite.berkeley.edu/InternetIndex/): A searchable, annotated subject directory of more than 5,300 Internet resources selected and evaluated by librarians for their usefulness to users of public libraries.

Internet Realities

Web sites may be down or dead. Anywhere from five to twenty percent of the sites listed in your search results will be inaccessible, either because the computer where the site resides is "down," the site address has changed and you don't know the new one, your server doesn't like the other server, or the site itself has simply vanished. Faced with any of these situations, you may try accessing the site at a later time and hope its computer is "up," or you may try conducting another search with the information you have about the site. But it may well be that the site simply doesn't exist anymore. Web sites come and go; they emerge, grow, and change addresses. This is particularly the case with Web sites belonging to individuals or small organizations. This may well be a tragedy, but it is also a reality.

Books go out of print and magazine runs cease, but the paper in them survives and we may use the text in our research for decades, or even centuries, after it first appeared. But when a Web site vanishes, it is as if it never existed in the first place. Researchers need to keep this in mind. Make a paper copy of interesting content wherever possible. By the time you finish your research, that Web site may no longer exist.

While it seems banal to characterize the Web as constantly changing, it is a truth that must be emphasized. Remember, too, that change often extends beyond mere content volume. It encompasses issues such as how we can find information on the Web, what kinds of information are available, what is free and what is not, and how the information is delivered to us. It is reasonable to assume that much of what you knew about the Internet a year ago might well be wrong now. This may make the prospect of "figuring out" the Internet appear hopeless, but keep in mind that it also means we have still not realized the full potential of the Internet. The tools and resources currently available are enormous; what comes later may be even more wondrous.

Using Email—"Netiquette"

Contacting other researchers for information and other research assistance via email is easy and very useful. Many researchers may be willing to help you out with your research, but it is important to keep the following points in mind:

- Be open about who you are and why you need the information.
- If you're looking for answers to specific questions, be sure to check some of the obvious sources first. Don't burden other researchers with simple questions like "What year did Dazzy Vance retire?" that can be answered using standard baseball reference sources.
- If you're asking for information to support your own research, especially if your work is part of a commercial venture (such as for a book you're writing, or a commercial Web site), you should be up front with other researchers about it and ask their permission to use the information they provide.
- Always credit your source. If Researcher X supplies you with information you end up using for your published work, you should acknowledge that debt.

These are basic rules for any research project, but you should not lose sight of them simply because you are using email and cannot see or hear the folks you are writing to.

A few years back, a cartoon in *The New Yorker* showed two dogs working on a computer. One dog says to the other, "On the Internet, no one knows you're a dog." This joke points up the attractive anonymity offered by the Internet. No one need know who you are, where you are, or anything else about you. For some people, this anonymity seems to open the door to irresponsible behavior. That is unfortunate. When using email, particularly with online discussion groups, you should always remember that your words are being read by other living, breathing, human beings with their own thoughts and feelings that can be hurt or offended.

Popping off (flaming), sarcasm, or insults are rarely justifiable. Even humor should be used carefully with people you don't know. Remember that you don't have the benefit of verbal inflection, gestures, or facial expressions with email. Your joke may be lost on your audience, or even be taken the wrong way. This not to suggest you can never use humor or send messages in anything but the most formal language. Simply keep in mind that you may be addressing strangers and that you should treat them with the same respect as if you were meeting them in person for the first time. For more information on netiquette, try the Web Style site at www.sun.com/styleguide/.

Perhaps because of its impermanent, non-intrusive nature, email appears even easier to ignore than junk mail. It also has a delivery failure rate worse than the postal service's. If you send a message to someone asking for a response and you do not receive one within a few days, don't hesitate to send your original message again.

Reliability of Online Resources

It is easy and cheap to set up a Web site on the Internet. This is attractive to many users, but consider what it implies about the Internet as an information resource. If anyone can have a Web site, then any kind of "information" can find its way onto the Web. Verifying "facts" in printed sources is sometimes a necessary part of research. When the "facts" come off the Web, verification is imperative. Start by identifying the original source. If you find the information in a document associated with a known organization or otherwise credible source (e.g., the New York *Times*, the Center for Disease Control, Virginia Commonwealth University), then the information is more likely to be reliable, though as a researcher, you will always want to verify. If you find it on an unknown individual's Web site, or a Web site associated with an organization having nothing to do with baseball or sports, you need to be more careful. With no editorial policy governing the content of Web sites, the potential for nonsense or falsehood is high.

Fee vs. Free

The idea that everything is free on the Internet is almost as ludicrous as the idea that one can find anything and everything on the Internet. The great majority of Web sites are free, but many of the indexes, databases, and full-text resources you are likely to use in your research are not free—at least not from your home computer. Many are available for free at libraries with specific licensing agreements, but some may be accessed only by *by Clifford Otto / SABR Webmaster*

SABR is working to expand its Web site, and in the future a good bit of SABR material will almost certainly be written with the site in mind. Here is a little information about the technical side of writing for the Web.

HTML (Hypertext Markup Language) is a set of computer instructions designed to control the layout and appearance of Web pages, but there is wide latitude in the elements supported, depending on your browser.

If you start your word processor and compose your article using all its fancy features (bulleted lists; indented paragraphs; underlining, boldface, and italics; curlicued quotation marks and apostrophes; superscript, etc.), these will all get lost when your file is converted into text, and the Webmaster will have to add all the tags that separate paragraphs, boldface text, and so on.

One way to make the Webmaster's task easier, and to preserve the formatting you want, is to learn a bit of HTML yourself—four simple tags that control text appearance and paragraph layout. When you have finished, be sure to save it as a text (.txt) file.

The three most common enhancements to text are boldface, italics, and underlining. HTML coding uses simple pairs of switches to turn these features on and off: <B> **turns on boldface type and** </B> turns it off. <I> *turns on italics, and* </I> turns it off. <U> <u>turns on underlining and</u> </U> turns it off. These tags can be nested. For example, to get underlined bold italics, you simply write <U><B><I> <u>***text to appear this way***</u> </I></B></U>. The order of application is not important, but the relative relationship of the enhancements is. Also, you should avoid extraneous spaces. Another piece of HTML code you may find useful is the paragraph marker pair, <P></P>. Place the <P> at the beginning of a paragraph and the </P> at the end.

Tables present a special problem for Webmasters because it is very time-consuming to convert a printed table into its HTML equivalent. One way to simplify things is to write your tables using a delimiter to separate columnar data. Use a character that does not appear in your data, such as a semicolon. For example: Year;AB;R;H;2B can automatically be converted to a table, while Year AB R H 2B would have to be converted by hand.

Newer versions of word processors have the ability to convert documents to HTML, but they generally produce very sloppy coding that often requires as much work to clean up as would be needed to code from scratch.

Preparing pictures for the Web: Unless you know what you are doing, let the Webmaster do the job. There are many pitfalls to be avoided, such as file formats, optimization, and web-safe color. Either send the original picture for the Webmaster to scan, or if you scan it yourself, save the file in a "non-lossy" format—.tif, .png, .bmp, or .psd. File sizes increase by the square, so if you scan the picture yourself, use a scanner resolution of 72-100 dpi. Use the maximum color capability that your scanner supports.

paying a fee. It may turn out that your information source comes from a fee-based site. Be prepared to pay for what you need.

SEARCHING TIPS: *Keywords, Free-text, and "Natural Language"*

Library catalogs, indexes of magazine articles, and the like use uniform systems of terms and headings to help researchers locate materials on a given subject. Uniformity is the key here. Let's say you're looking for something about Babe Ruth. Do you look up "Babe Ruth" or "Ruth, Babe" or "George Herman Ruth?" A good catalog or index will have all materials related to the Babe under a single heading, so you don't have to worry about checking them all. Using a catalog or index, you will know that every reference to Babe Ruth will have some information about him, rather than a passing mention.

With a keyword or "free-text" search, however, you have no uniformity. If you type in "Babe Ruth" you will not necessarily get materials that identify him as "George Herman Ruth" or "The Babe" or "The Sultan of Swat" and so on. You will, however, get absolutely everything containing the name "Babe Ruth," even if it is completely trivial or has nothing whatever to do with the Babe. This is not to suggest that catalogs and indexes are always better than keyword searches. Sometimes this sort of comprehensiveness is an advantage over the selective nature of catalogs and indexes. At other times it is a burden. The important point is that you be aware of these differences.

"Natural language" searching (or NLP—natural language programming) is intended to free the searcher from worrying about how to phrase whatever it is he or she is looking for. Let's say you want to know how much Babe Ruth's bat weighed. Using a "natural language" search engine, such as Ask Jeeves (www.askjeeves.com), you might type in "How much did Babe Ruth's bat weigh?" as if you were asking the question of another person. What the search engine does is to strip down the question, focusing on the terms Babe, Ruth, Bat, and Weigh. The natural-language search engine responds with Web sites not only about Babe Ruth but also about bats (those flying mammals), weight-loss programs, and baseball bats having nothing to do with Babe Ruth. You will also be shown Web sites about George Herman Ruth, many of them having nothing to do with the thrust of your question, the weight of his bat. Still, amid the welter of information, you may find precisely the answer you're looking for. A more efficient approach, though, might be to combine the terms that describe your research topic in a way likely to produce better results. This more efficient way may involve Boolean logic.

Search Operators

With most electronic catalogs and indexes, the best way to search is by using search operators. These are words (often called Boolean operators, after the English logician George Boole) that combine, differentiate, or exclude key terms in your search. Using search operators allows you to . . .

❷ group related terms;

❷ combine different terms to obtain a result sharing both terms, or

❷ exclude a term or terms from your search set.

While the problem of separating the wheat from the chaff still holds, learning to use these search operators can help you focus in on the information you need. Search operators are usually confined to three words: AND, OR, and NOT. These words, or operators, can be used in relation to the terms that are essential to your research.

With AND you are looking for materials containing both terms: *baseball* AND *bat*: This will give you materials that contain both terms. It will not give you materials containing one term but not the other.

With OR you are looking for materials containing either term: *baseball* OR *football*. With NOT you are looking for materials containing the first term, but not the second term: *baseball* NOT *football*: This choice will give you materials containing the term *baseball*, eliminating any item that contains the term *football*. Note that the use of NOT will exclude all materials containing the word *football*, even if they contain the word *baseball* as well. For this reason, it pays to be cautious when using the NOT operator.

Boolean operators are not an option with many Internet search engines. But don't despair. There is a familiar pair of symbols that will help you to improve your chances when looking for information. Instead of the AND and OR Boolean operators, most search engines use plus (+) and minus (-) to combine or exclude terms. Phrases (that is, two or more words, such as Babe Ruth) must be enclosed in quotation marks to show that they form a unit. To return to the example of Babe Ruth's bat weight, you might try...

```
+"babe ruth"  +weighed  +bat
```

Notice that there is no space between the plus and the terms, but that there are spaces between the terms themselves [i.e., +"babe ruth" /space/+weighed/space/+bat]. The use of this method produced helpful information with the first few Web sites in search results when using the Alta Vista and Fast search engines. It isn't a cure-all, but it is a useful technique. Carefully selecting and combining your search terms is generally more productive than "natural language" searching.

Organizational Resources

If you know the information source you are looking for, by all means skip search engines and go directly to the organization that produced it; for example, the *Total Baseball* site for player statistics, or the New York *Times* for a recent column by George Vecsey. An easy tip for finding organizational sites is to use the organization's name itself. Simply bracket the name between "www." and ".com" (or ".org," if it's a nonprofit). For example: www.chicagotribune.com, www.totalbaseball.com, www.baseballhalloffame.org, www.majorleaguebaseball.com, or www.stats.com.

Your guesses will be right half the time, and this will save the time of burrowing through the results of a search engine search. But if that doesn't work, a good search engine for locating organizational sites is currently Google (www.google.com).

Authority Files

In the case of many electronic catalogs and indexes, you will have the advantage of browsing a directory of the terms used in order to find the correct usage. For example, if you are looking for articles on baseball players and drug abuse, do you look them up under "drug abuse" or "drugs" or "chemical dependency"? An authority list will give you the specific term used by that catalog or index. Generally speaking, whenever possible, it is better to use subject headings to look up your information in catalogs and indexes than to use keywords or free-text.

ELECTRONIC DATA RESOURCES: Libraries

As mentioned in Chapter 2, libraries are likely to be your main source for printed information pertinent to your research. This continues to be the case with electronic data resources. The most salient feature of the computer world facing the researcher is the fact that nearly all library catalogs are now on computer. The protestations of Nicholson Baker and others notwithstanding (see Baker's "The Annals of Scholarship: Discards" in *The New Yorker* of April 4, 1994), putting the catalog on computer has been a boon to library users. The computerized or "online" library catalog allows for far more rapid and flexible searching than past formats, including the beloved/loathed card catalog. Thousands of public and academic library catalogs are also accessible over the Internet. Those that are Web-based are generally the easiest to use. Among them, the following are of particular significance to the baseball researcher. (When www does not appear in an Internet address, the user types the address immediately after http:// on the address line.)

- ❶ Library of Congress (www.loc.gov)
- ❶ New York Public Library (catnyp.nypl.org)
- ❶ Cleveland Public Library (www.cpl.org)
- ❶ Boston Public Library (www.bpl.org)
- ❶ Family History Library (www.familysearch.org/Search/searchcatalog.asp)
- ❶ Smithsonian Institution Libraries (www.sil.si.edu/newstart.htm)
- ❶ Detroit Public Library (www.detroit.lib.mi.us)
- ❶ Berkeley Digital Library Image Library (sunsite.berkeley.edu/ImageFinder)
- ❶ Genealogical Library Master Catalog
  (www.ancestry.com/ancestry/search/3622.htm)

Directories of Online Library Catalogs:

- ❼ **WEBCATS** (www.lights.com/webcats/) A fine directory for locating many Web-based library catalogs.
- ❼ **Libweb** (sunsite.berkeley.edu/Libweb) Lists over 3,000 Web-pages from libraries in over ninety countries.

The researcher should be aware not only of the online catalog of his or her local library but also the online catalogs of other local public library systems, colleges, and universities. Consortium catalogs are of great importance, too. These are unified catalogs encompassing dozens, even hundreds, of public or academic and special libraries over a small or large geographic area. For example, **MNLink** (www.mnlink.org) is a union catalog to hundreds of public, academic, and special library catalogs throughout the state of Minnesota. You can search the holdings of all these libraries from a single search screen. Statewide consortia such as this one are becoming increasingly common. Another advantage of using library consortia is that by pooling resources they are often able to afford the licensing of many online indexing and full-text sources.

The king of all online union catalogs, however, is OCLC's WorldCat. (OCLC stands for Online Computer Library Center, a nonprofit organization that provides cataloging and information services, mainly for libraries.) OCLC's WorldCat records the holdings of several thousand libraries in the U.S. and Canada, encompassing many millions of books, serials, recordings, and other library materials. In addition to providing data about each library item, it displays the all-important "holdings" information. This tells you which libraries have copies of the source you are looking for. It should come as no surprise that OCLC is the principal resource used by Interlibrary Loan services (ILL) in public and academic libraries. Using OCLC's WorldCat (available through the FirstSearch service at public and academic libraries), researchers can find the holdings for millions of titles.

Of related interest are directories to archival holdings. There are several fine online directories, but except for NUCMC, which is freely accessible, these directories are proprietary databases that must be accessed through the libraries that subscribe to them.

- ❼ **National Union Catalog of Manuscript Collections** (NUCMC) A cooperative cataloging service operated by the Library of Congress for archival collections. (lcweb.loc.gov/coll/nucmc/nucmc.html)
- ❼ **ArchivesUSA**. Holdings and contact information of more than 4,800 collections. Indexes to over 109,000 special collections. Proprietary data, but often available through academic libraries.
- ❼ **Archival Resources**. Includes over 500,000 collection records and nearly 7,000 collection guides. Proprietary data, often available through academic libraries.

PROPRIETARY DATA: DATABASES, INDEXES, AND "FULL-TEXT"

As noted earlier, a great many resources are available online, but not all of them are free. Even some that are free can be used only at libraries that are licensed by the publishers or vendors to make the data available to their patrons. For example, a periodicals index such as **ABI Inform** is not available to everyone to search for free. However, a large public library, an academic library, or a library consortium may contract with the vendor of this database to make it available to in-house library users or via remote access to registered library patrons (or students and faculty, in the case of academic libraries). The researcher is well advised to explore what indexes and databases are available not only through the local library but also at academic libraries and through library consortia in the area.

CD-ROM, Web-based, and Online Databases

Until about ten years ago, electronic indexes worked in much the same way as their paper-based predecessors. Searching them was much faster and more accurate, and they offered some additional information, but they were still essentially "bibliographic" databases. They told you what had been written about your research topic but did not give you the actual text of the sources. Most databases today, however, have at least some full-text component. That is to say, you get not only the information about the article or document, you get the complete text as well—sometimes even the images.

For several years, many of these databases have been available on CD-ROM, but that medium has since largely given way to Web-based platforms. The following vendors carry hundreds, even thousands, of bibliographic and full-text databases on all subjects. Access to these may require a librarian to do the searching for you, but they are usually accessible at most public and academic libraries.

Database Vendors:

- **DIALOG**: Longtime vendor of several hundred bibliographic, full-text, and newspaper databases. Fee-based service, but available through many public and academic libraries.
- **OCLC's FirstSearch**: Access to eighty-five online databases and more than five million full-text articles. Fee-based service, but available through many public and academic libraries.
- **Lexis/Nexis Academic Universe**: The online information giant with business, academic, legal, and government data services. Most useful to baseball researchers for its full-text access to the New York *Times* and the huge Lexis legal database. Available through some large public and academic libraries.

Newspapers

Nearly all major American newspapers not only have Web sites, they also allow access to their archives. For most of them, you can read about half of today's newspaper right from their Web site, and you can search for recent articles using a fairly crude search device. "Archives" refers to the cumulative holdings of the newspaper's articles in electronic form. In some cases, this material goes back to the early 1980s or before. The search engines are usually still quite limited, but they can give ready access to a decade or two of articles. The catch is that full-text articles usually aren't free, especially if you're accessing the sites from your home. But let's say you've found what you need in the Macon, Georgia, newspaper from the computer in your home in San Francisco. Paying a $1.50 fee for the article is probably preferable to any other option.

At many libraries, the articles from some newspapers are free if you're viewing them at the library. Vendors may have licensing agreements with libraries allowing their patrons full-text access for on-site searches. It should also be noted that many newspapers from smaller cities, such as the Duluth *News-Tribune*, are available on the Web, often with archives. AJR NewsLink (ajr.newslink.org/news.html) is an excellent directory to hundreds of newspaper sites in the U.S. and abroad. Other notable newspapers on the Web are...

- New York *Times* (archives.nytimes.com/archives): Full-text for some recent articles.
- Los Angeles *Times* (www.latimes.com/HOME/ARCHIVES): Searchable archives from 1990-present; full-text available for fee only.
- Chicago *Tribune* (www.chicagotribune.com/tools/search/archives/archives.htm): Searchable archives from 1985-present; full-text available for fee only.
- Boston *Globe* (www.boston.com/globe/search): Searchable archives from 1981-present; full-text available for fee only.
- USA *Today* (archives.usatoday.com) Searchable archives from 1987-present; full-text available for fee only.
- Washington *Post* (www.washingtonpost.com/wp-adv/archives/front.htm) Searchable archives from 1986-present; full-text available for fee only.

Magazines

Full-text magazine articles are becoming increasingly common. Not long ago, most magazines provided online indexes only, but now all online general periodical indexes routinely have a full-text option for about half of their indexed publications. For example, *Sports Illustrated*, *The Sporting News*, and *USA Today Baseball Weekly* have been in full-text for the past few years. Don't make any assumptions, though. There are many sports magazines that are neither on the Web nor electronically indexed, much less available in full-text. Among these are *Sports Collectors Digest, Sport, Baseball Digest, Baseball America, Nine, Spitball, Beckett's Sports Card Monthly*, not to mention a host of local and small press publications. In fact, you will find that sports publications are generally given short shrift by most general periodical indexes, even though these indexes usually cover well over a thousand titles. But don't stop with newspapers and sports publications when doing your research. "Non-sport" publications—news magazines, educational, business, medical, legal, or whatever—sometimes have considerable coverage of baseball and can provide important information. One or more of the following online general periodical indexes are commonly available even at small local libraries.

- **InfoTrac SearchBank**: Indexes over a thousand magazine titles back to 1980. Some recent articles are in full-text.
- **EBSCO**: MasterFile version covers over 1,800 titles from 1984-present; full-text from 1990-present.
- **ProQuest Direct**: Indexes over 1,600 magazine titles, some back to the 1970s. Some recent articles available in full-text.
- **Carl UnCover**: Covers over 18,000 multidisciplinary journals. Contains brief descriptive information for over 8,800,000 articles since Fall, 1988.
- **Current Contents**: Articles, reviews, letters, notes, and editorials from more than 7,500 scholarly journals. 1994-present.
- **Expanded Academic Index**: Approximately 1,580 scholarly and general interest periodicals, including the latest six months of the New York *Times*. 1980-present.
- **Inside Information Plus**: 21,000 current journals, many citations also contain abstracts. 1996-present.

Then there are a host of other specialty indexes available from library sites. University libraries often have made dozens of these indexes available through their library catalogs at on-campus locations. Most of the specialty indexes still do not provide full-text, but even knowing that something exists is an important first step. Here is a sampling of some of the many subject- specific databases available on CD-ROM and over the Web. Many are available at large public or academic libraries. Those with Web addresses shown are accessible free from anywhere.

- **ABI Inform**: Business articles from over 1,000 periodicals, many in full-text; 1971-present.
- **AJR NewsLink**: (ajr.newslink.org) Links to dozens of periodical Web sites.
- **American City Business Journals**: (www.amcity.com) Full-text articles from forty local business journals (e.g., *City Business*) back to 1996.
- **ATLA Religion Database**: Index to religious periodicals; 1949-present.

O **Arts and Humanities Citation Index**: Index to over 1,000 arts and humanities periodicals; 1980-present.

O **Avery Index to Architectural Periodicals**: Index to over 1,000 architectural periodicals; 1977-present.

O **Black Studies Database**: Index to journals, magazines, newspapers, newsletters, pamphlets, and reports published 1948-1986.

O **Chicano Database**: Index to books and articles in both English and Spanish; 1967-1993.

O **Dissertation Abstracts**: Bibliographic citations for older titles. Abstracts for dissertations since 1980 and for masters' theses since 1988; 1861-present.

O **ERIC**: (ericae.net/main.htm) Nearly a million references to thousands of educational topics. Includes journal articles, books, theses, curricula, conference papers, standards, guidelines, and other documents; 1966-present.

O **Ethnic Newswatch**: News articles on all subjects in the newspapers, magazines, and journals of the ethnic, minority, and native press; 1990-present.

O **General Business File**: Over 900 English language business and trade publications, full text for 460 titles; 1982-present.

O **General Science Abstracts**: Indexes 140 "core" science journals; 1984-present.

O **Grateful Med**: (igm.nlm.nih.gov) Index to several health-related periodicals and documents, including *Medlines* (back to 1960s).

O **Hispanic American Periodicals Index**: Indexes articles in more than 400 scholarly journals published in Latin America or treating Latin American and U.S. Hispanic topics; 1970-present.

O **PAIS International**: Indexes a potpourri of articles, books, conference proceedings, government documents, book chapters, statistical directories, reports of public and private agencies, materials from the U. S. Congress; 1972-present.

O **Periodicals Contents Index**: (PCI Web) Bibliographic citations from the tables of contents of a growing number of journals. Currently indexes over 7.5 million articles in 1,977 journals from the seventeenth century to 1991.

O **PsycINFO**: Indexes articles from over 1,300 journals in psychology and related fields; 1967-present.

O **Sociological Abstracts**: Indexes journal articles, conference proceedings and papers, dissertations, research reviews, and monographs; 1963-present.

O **SportDiscus**: A bibliographic database with international coverage of journal articles but also includes Web sites, books, book chapters, conference proceedings, dissertations, and theses, 1949-present. Most of the coverage is on physical fitness and sports medicine.

- **Sports Illustrated**: (CNNSI.com/features/cover/archive) Full-text from 1998 to the present for most articles; includes illustrations/photos.
- **Statistical Universe**: Online version of the *American Statistics Index*, from 1973 (U.S.); *Statistical Reference Index*, from 1980 (U.S. and other); *Index to International Statistics*, from 1983.
- **USA Today Baseball Weekly**: (www.usatoday.com/bbwfront.htm) Click on current issue. This will bring up a page with links to back files containing issues from January 1997 to the present. Free.

Miscellaneous Sources:

- **Biography and Genealogy Master Index** (BGMI): Over 12 million biographical references from eighty biographical reference sources spanning more than twenty years.
- **Biography Source**: Biographical sketches on over 150,000 individuals from hundreds of sources.
- **FamilySearch**: (www.familysearch.org) Ancestor search service. Free.
- **Social Security Death Index**: (www.ancestry.com/ssdi/advanced.htm) Search over 60 million names.
- **Intellectual Property Network**: (www.patents.ibm.com) Includes partial full-text and full-image of all United States patents from 1971-present. Good search interface.

Books:

Apart from library catalogs and other research collections, there are several directories of use to the researcher. The old print standard is also available at many libraries as a CD-ROM or through FirstSearch.

Books in Print

- **Amazon Books**: (www.amazon.com) This darling of cyberbusiness has a large database of titles and offers a handy way to check publication status, publisher, ISBN, pagination, and price.
- **Barnes & Noble**: (www.bn.com) A competitor to Amazon in the sale of new books, B&N also has an out-of-print, used-book feature that connects you with the holdings of hundreds of used book dealers.
- **ABEBooks**: (www.abebooks.com) Another used book dealer site. Includes many rare books.
- **Bookfinder**: (www.bookfinder.com) Another used book dealer site.

Baseball Sites

The number of baseball sites is growing continuously and now numbers in the thousands. There is hardly space to address more than a handful here, but below are some excellent directories along with a few specific sites that cover most, if not all, that are noteworthy.

- **John Skilton's Baseball Links** (www.baseball-links.com): Touted as "The Web's most comprehensive collection of links to baseball resources." 6,022 links as of November, 1999. Indexed by about twenty broad categories. A very handy directory.

- **Sean Lahman's Baseball Links** (www.baseball1.com): Lots of links, as with the Skilton site, but has a strong emphasis on current news and statistics (modern and historical). Includes free, downloadable database with basic statistics on all major league players, past and present.

- **SABR Members' Web Sites and Pages** (www.sabr.org/links.shtml): A directory of links that reflects the broad interests of SABR members. There's everything here from the sublime to the slightly ridiculous, much of it interesting as well as useful.

- **Total Baseball** (www.totalbaseball.com) Partial statistical information on players and teams. Free, easy-to-use historical source.

- ***Baseball on the Web* by Rob Edelman** (IDG Books Worldwide, 1998.): A book? Yes, indeed. Edelman's book provides excellent reviews of hundreds of sites current at the time for those of you who are more comfortable reviewing a list in print than one on the Web. John Benson is scheduled to have another book on this subject out in 2000 (*Benson's Guide to Baseball on the Internet*). Both Edelman and Benson are SABR members.

- **The Baseball Index** (formerly known as RBI) (www. sabrrbi@baldeagle.com): This is an index to baseball literature developed by SABR's Bibliography Committee. It is also an ongoing project to catalog the entirety of baseball literature from the earliest references to the present day. It is by far the largest index to baseball literature in existence and can serve as an excellent source of information for many kinds of baseball research projects.

Started in 1992, the The Baseball Index database has grown to over 130,000 records of books, articles, songs, poems, short stories, cartoons, advertisements, and other materials. As with most indexes, it records bibliographic data about each source:

- Author	- Document type	- Publication/Publisher name
- Title	- Named person(s)	- Copyright/Issue dates
- Statistical content	- Topic(s)	- Pagination
- Illustration content	- Content notes	- Volume/Issue number
		- Other bibliographic data

The Baseball Index is accessible two ways—either by purchasing the entire database, or by sending your search request to the The Baseball Index Data Service. The full database is a computer file searchable using any of a number of commercially available programs. The database is delivered on a CD-ROM disk and the file is copied to the hard drive of the researcher's home computer. The Baseball Index is available as a one-time purchase or on a subscription basis. SABR members enjoy a substantial discount. More information on purchasing can be found at the SABR Web site (www.sabr.org/merchandise/rbi.shtml).

Alternatively, The Baseball Index Data Service will search The Baseball Index database for specific sources. Researchers submit their research request (e.g., "I am researching baseball during World War II") via email or post. The database is searched and the researcher is informed of the number of sources located (e.g., "The Baseball Index lists 256 source references on baseball during World War II"). For a modest fee, the researcher can then purchase a list of these sources, which are delivered either via email or as a mailed printout. More information on The Baseball Index Data Service can be found at the SABR Web site (www.sabr.org/dataserv.shtml).

Requests may be sent to The Baseball Index, 3536 Orchard Lane, Minnetonka MN 55305, or to the Index Web site (sabrrbi@baldeagle.com).

All revenues go to support SABR and its mission. The Baseball Index is owned by SABR and is an entirely volunteer effort.

Chapter Five

SABERMETRICS

by Neal Traven

It's startling to observe that the term *sabermetrics* never appeared in 1987's *Baseball Research Handbook*, the direct antecedent of this volume. Bill James, whose increasingly popular *Bill James Baseball Annual* had been published by Ballantine since 1982, merited one oblique reference. John Thorn and Pete Palmer's 1984 book *The Hidden Game of Baseball*, a seminal history of the development of baseball statistics and full explication of Palmer's Linear Weights methodology, is completely absent from the *Handbook*. Then again, way back in 1987 few people possessed much computational power and fewer still had access to large baseball datasets.

In the decade-plus since *The Baseball Research Handbook* appeared, the baseball world has been inundated with numbers. In *USA Today Baseball Weekly*, *Sports Illustrated*, and other mainstream publications, we no longer see just the traditional stats like batting average, RBIs, ERA, wins, and losses. Baseball telecasts routinely inform us about a player's situational stats, the more abstruse the better ("Joe is a career .333 hitter with one out and runners at the corners in the late innings of night games against crafty lefthanders born west of the Mississippi"). If Peter Gammons of ESPN talks about OPS (On-base percentage Plus Slugging percentage), it must be entering common baseball parlance. The availability of minutely detailed information about every pitch of every game, the explosion of fantasy leagues and record-keeping services to support them, and the increasing interest in baseball data analysis have all contributed to the burgeoning popularity of baseball statistics.

This chapter discusses the scope of sabermetrics as a form of baseball research. Following a discussion of some of the issues of interest to sabermetricians, it outlines and describes a variety of sources of information about the methodologies and results of sabermetric research. While the chapter is in no way a cookbook for "how to do sabermetrics," it is my hope that an overview of what sabermetricians do, why they do it, and what tools they use will be valuable to SABR members who have an interest in delving into this field of research.

AN OVERVIEW OF SABERMETRICS

Sabermetrics is both similar to and different from other forms of baseball research. Like other research disciplines, sabermetric research is a process of defining the issue of interest, reviewing the literature, formulating a working hypothesis about the subject, collecting and analyzing the requisite data, writing a report of the findings, and sharing those results with others. The primary difference between sabermetric research and the preponderance of baseball research is between their models of research methodology.

The work of SABR committees such as Biography, Negro Leagues, Oral History, and so forth usually follows the humanities/history model—searching for original information sources, such as interviews, letters, contracts, photographs, and the like, in order to document an historical event or build a coherent biography of a subject. The researcher's task is to locate and assess as much original source material as possible, digging through libraries and newspaper archives, interviewing participants and relatives, separating fact from fiction from apocrypha. The writer weaves the facts and information disclosed by the investigation into an essay that interprets and elucidates the meaning and cogency of the events depicted. In contrast, sabermetrics usually follows the approach of scientific (or perhaps social science) research, concentrating on numeric data that can be summarized using statistical procedures, developing and refining hypotheses by testing them against large numeric datasets. This analytic approach can be applied to off-the-field subjects such as baseball economics, but it is most often used to analyze events on the field—singles and saves, steals and triples, outs and walks, bunting and clutch hitting.

In *The Bill James Historical Baseball Abstract*, James defines sabermetrics as "the search for objective knowledge about baseball." This definition may overstate the case somewhat, for not all objective information about baseball is fodder for sabermetrics. In reality, sabermetricians are usually interested in examining the collected record of the events that take place on the field of play, attempting to learn how these events interrelate with each other, and to build empirical models describing the regularities uncovered in that search. In other words, the "objective knowledge" sought by sabermetricians is that which characterizes and contributes to baseball offense and defense.

Focus on Scoring

The statistical record of baseball is more voluminous and more comprehensive than that of any other sport. An extensive record of the competing teams' efforts on offense and defense is found in the play-by-play scoring of each game. These game records are summed across the entire season to produce the player and team season statistics appearing in baseball encyclopedias and similar databases, and player-seasons are summed to build the career totals in the same databases. Depending on the specific topic of inquiry, a sabermetrician will want to examine the data at one or more of these levels of summarization.

Perhaps the fundamental tenet of the sabermetric method is the primacy of runs. Runs are the currency of baseball; the goal of offense (batting and baserunning) is to score runs and the goal of defense (pitching and fielding) is to prevent the other side from scoring runs. The team whose combined offense and defense has done the better job of achieving its goal at the end of the contest is the winner of the game. If runs are baseball's currency, outs are the equivalent of the clock in a sport like football or basketball. Each half-inning lasts until the offensive team has consumed three outs, and the game ends when the trailing team has used up all of its allotted innings and the outs from which they were built.

Sabermetrics, then, is largely the study of what contributes to, is important for, or is associated with run-scoring (batting and base-running) and prevention of run-scoring (pitching and fielding). Most often, the unit of analysis is the individual player. We wish to assess the player's own value, independent of influences such as his ballpark or his teammates, which are beyond his control. This work includes evaluating the value of traditional measures such as batting average, RBIs, or wins and losses, as well as proposing alternative statistical measures designed to provide insights into the game that may not be evident in the traditional stats.

The Usefulness of a Statistic

As discussed in David Grabiner's Sabermetric Manifesto (baseball.com/bb-data/grabiner/manifesto.html), three questions must be addressed in order to assess the usefulness of a baseball statistic, whether it's a time-honored traditional one or a brand-new sabermetric one:

- ❶ Does the statistic measure an important contribution to its goal?
- ❷ How well does the statistic measure a player's own contribution?
- ❸ Is there a better way to measure the same thing?

These questions and similar ones posed by Bill James in 1987 and Phil Birnbaum in 1999 are important in evaluating baseball stats because of the difficulty, if not impossibility, of directly measuring the number of runs an individual player contributes. To illustrate, let's look at RBIs as a measure of offense. Many people see RBIs as a strong, perhaps even the strongest, indicator of run production. RBIs "want" to measure the runs a player contributes to his team, and thus Grabiner's first question receives a positive answer. But RBIs do rather poorly with respect to the second question, because they are too often credited to a player who clearly had little to do with the run. For example, consider this play-by-play sequence: Alfa leads off the inning with a walk, Bravo forces him at second, Charlie smacks a ground-rule double, Delta hits a sacrifice fly, Echo fans to end the inning. The team scored one run on a hit and a walk. Delta picked up the RBI and Bravo scored the run, yet in fact those two players may have been the most detrimental of the five batters in the inning, since they hit into two of the three outs in the inning. Charlie and Alfa were the players who avoided making outs, thereby building the team's potential for scoring, yet they received zero credit for the team's run.

Circumstances Alter Cases

Of course, that scenario was built specifically to display a false impression arising from using RBIs as a measure of a player's contribution to the offense. But the play-by-play sequence illustrated above certainly isn't outlandish or bizarre. Innings often look something like that, and the "wrong" players too often score or knock in runs.

A player's seasonal runs and RBIs are decidedly team-dependent, park-dependent, and batting order-dependent. On a team full of strong offensive performers, even a weak hitter may end up with a superficially impressive number of runs or RBIs. Just as Coors Field increases significantly the number of runs scored, so too do fields like Dodger and Shea Stadiums lower run-scoring. Playing half your games in an extreme park will affect the total number of runs tallied by the team. And of course a lead-off hitter is more likely to score runs knocked in by the heart of the lineup behind him than to drive in the weaker bottom-of-the-lineup hitters who bat immediately before him.

The "Top-Down" Strategy

If one cannot directly determine a player's contribution to the runs scored by his team, then what can be done? The sabermetric methodology is to use information about the player that can be directly measured, so as to estimate that contribution. This directly measurable information consists of such stats as hits, at bats, walks, steals, caught stealing, and so forth. In contrast to runs and RBIs, these accomplishments are minimally dependent on the player's teammates—a double is a two-base hit, whether the bases are empty or loaded. Using these quantities, weighted and combined empirically through the analysis of large datasets, the sabermetrician can construct a model to estimate the player's contribution to run-scoring.

To estimate a player's value in creating runs, then, the researcher's task is to combine the team-independent numbers in the player's statistical record in an accurate manner. But this brings us back to the problem of separating the individual's contributions from the context of his team—how can you evaluate the accuracy of the model without an independent validating criterion? What can you measure your estimate against, if you know in advance that run scoring is team-dependent?

One widely-applied approach begins at the level of the team. At the team-season level you can measure the relationship between the actual number of runs scored and a hypothesized equation composed of team-independent stats. That is because a team, unlike an individual player, is a complete system. There are no "other players" partially responsible for some portion of the runs scored by a team.

Thus, the validity of a model derived from a team's seasonal stats can be tested by comparing the number of runs predicted by the model against the actual number of runs scored by the team. In testing over a large number of observations (lots of teams, lots of years), models such as Bill James's Runs Created, Pete Palmer's Batting Runs, Clay Davenport's Equivalent Runs, Jim Furtado's Extrapolated Runs, and others have been shown to estimate a team's seasonal run total more accurately than do traditional summary stats like batting average. Though they differ in their details—specific categories of offensive events used, coefficients applied to the events, mathematical operations (such as addition, multiplication, etc.)—well-constructed models generally paint a consistent picture of baseball offense.

Applying these team-based models to individual players requires an inferential leap. A full-time player accumulates approximately as many plate appearances in a season as a team does in 15-18 games. Applying these models to a player's stats is equivalent to estimating the number of runs produced in that number of games by a lineup composed entirely of nine copies of the player. Because the models are validated using team statistics, it's quite possible that this inference is less accurate at the extremes than near the average. The best and worst teams are much more similar in their statistical profiles than are the best and worst players. Thus, we cannot be sure that associations validated over the relatively narrow distribution of team profiles can be extrapolated beyond that range. The primary tasks of offense are (a) getting on base and (b) advancing runners. In players who are particularly adept, or particularly deficient, at both skills, there is a potential interaction effect in the formulas. In essence, the equations are based on a scenario where, say, Barry Bonds comes to the plate with Barry Bonds on base, or Rey Ordonez bats with Rey Ordonez (not) on base. Much sabermetric discussion has gone into trying to account and adjust for potential problem areas such as this one.

The "Bottom-Up" Strategy

An alternative to the "top-down" strategy described above is what might be termed a "bottom-up" methodology. Based on analysis of very large play-by-play event databases, sabermetricians have constructed tables of the expected number of runs scored, given a specific base-out situation. There are 24 base-out situations—bases empty/1 out, runners on first and third/2 outs, and so forth—each with measurable probability of occurrence, each with measurable expected runs. It must be emphasized that these expected-runs tables say nothing about what might happen in any specific plate appearance. In the long run, taking into account thousands, if not millions, of plate appearances, the tables reflect what has happened in the past.

Sabermetric investigation of datasets of this type is still in its infancy. In theory, it may be possible to sum up a player's performance, plate appearance by plate appearance, and compare that against the sum of expected results of the same set of plate appearances.

Taking into account additional potentially important variables—pitching hand, inning, game, score, and more—would make such analyses much more complicated and difficult. Accurate and virtually complete play-by-play datasets are available, largely through Retrosheet, back to at least the early 1980s, and researchers like Tom Ruane, David Smith, and others have begun to develop methods for their analysis and interpretation.

At its heart, sabermetric research is about applying generalizations to specifics. The goal of the sabermetrician is to find a way to measure or describe the issue of interest in general terms, and then to observe how players or teams are distributed within the model. It is never appropriate to start by asking yourself, "How can I build a measure to see how good a player X is?" Instead, you build a general measure of player quality or performance, and then look to see how it assesses players X, Y, Z, and many more. In all cases, you need to justify the reasons for the coefficients in your model. The model is driven by the data, not vice versa.

Once you're satisfied with your model, make it known to others. Whether by direct email to other researchers, a message on SABR-L, submission to *By the Numbers* (the Statistical Analysis Committee's newsletter), or other means, publish your findings. When your model is out in public, expect criticism, often pointed, and expect to be challenged. In explaining and exploring the reasoning behind your assumptions and methods, you may find guidance to refine and revise your model. Furthermore, others may find concepts and approaches in your work that will aid their research efforts. The sabermetric community can be brutal to those who cannot or will not engage and address critiques, particularly when the models appear to be arbitrary or the author argues from authority ("because I say so") without evincing supporting evidence. Conversely, sabermetricians are collegial and supportive to those who can back up their reasoning with data and are willing to listen and learn as much as they speak.

TOOLS OF THE TRADE

While it may be a slight overstatement to say that a personal computer is absolutely indispensable to a sabermetrician, it's difficult to see how one would be able to collect, maintain, study, analyze, and keep track of the volume of data used in most sabermetric analyses without a computer. On the other hand, the technology is not necessary for the conceptual thought processes surrounding the actual analyses. Defining the issues for study, proposing testable hypotheses, suggesting potential confounders or other barriers, evaluating whether the results of an analysis are reasonable, probing for possible flaws in the analytic logic, describing improvements and extensions to a completed analysis…all of these aspects of sabermetric research involve logical and empirical thinking that's outside the bailiwick of computers.

In summary, the computer is an almost obligatory but certainly not a sufficient tool for sabermetric research.

Hardware

With apologies to Macintosh enthusiasts, I know nothing about that segment of the computer market. Surely there are Macintosh computers capable of just about anything that can be done on a Windows machine, but I can't offer any advice about them.

When it comes to Windows machines, anything you can buy today will have more than enough storage space on its hard drive. Get plenty of horsepower (64 megabytes of RAM is a bare minimum, but go for at least 128 MB if you can afford it) and the fastest means you can find to connect to the Internet and World Wide Web. My cable modem is much, much faster than the 56K modem I used to have.

Software

For nearly all of your analytic needs, a spreadsheet such as Microsoft's Excel offers everything you need for sabermetric data analysis—data import and export, formula and equation building, built-in macros for basic statistical analysis, and graphical charts. Be sure to check the spreadsheet's maximum number of rows and columns. With up to 1,200 players in MLB each year, it would take less than fifteen seasons' worth of player data to exceed the limit of 16,384 rows in Excel for Windows 3.1. The Windows 95/98-based Excel97 can handle four times as many rows, but even its maximum of 65,536 rows might not handle much more than two thirds of a century of player-seasons. Another rather quirky limitation of Excel, at least through Excel97, is that it is incapable of handling dates before 1900. No Y2K problem in Excel97, but it does have a Y1899 bug!

More advanced handling of data is done with database software. Microsoft Access is the industry leader. Its point-and-click approach allows the user to build elaborate queries, pulling variables from several tables, applying conditions and criteria, and operating on the resulting information sets. MS Access is the native format of Sean Lahman's baseball data archive, and that in itself may be sufficient reason to learn how to use the software. For more intensive analysis and modeling, there are many high-powered statistical software systems on the market. Those few who really need packages like SPSS, SAS, or Mathematica will be willing to pay the high cost for them.

KNOWLEDGE BASE AND TRAINING

Do you have to be a statistician to do sabermetrics? In a word, no. Although some sabermetricians are trained in, or well-versed in, the academic discipline of statistics, the analysis and evaluation of baseball data is rarely anywhere near as erudite an endeavor as formal statistics.

In most cases, the software you're using will be capable of carrying out a wide variety of statistical procedures on the data you're examining. In sabermetrics, it's more important to know which type of procedure to use and when it's appropriate to use it than to know the full details of the equations behind the procedure. In fact, it's probably more important to be able to recognize when not to use a powerful formula that's available in your spreadsheet program but is inappropriate to the analysis you're building.

STATISTICAL CONCEPTS

To understand sabermetrics, you need to be aware of and comfortable with a number of general statistical concepts:

Central Tendency

Central tendency is a measure of the "typical" or "average" value of a set of observations. There are a number of ways to describe central tendency. The most common such measure is the mean, calculated by adding up all the values in the distribution and dividing by the number of observed values. This, of course, is what most people think of as the "average" of the distribution. If you order all of the observations from lowest to highest value, the median is the one where half the values are lower and half are higher. These two measures of central tendency are often similar, particularly when the distribution is something like a bell-shaped curve with most of the observations somewhere near the middle. But there are situations when these two indicators of centrality give very different results. Imagine the increase in the mean income of SABR members if Bill Gates were to join the organization! That unlikely event would have little effect on the median, since adding one more member to SABR might result in something like the median being the 3,354th highest income instead of the 3,353rd highest.

Variability

A second important statistical concept in sabermetrics is variability. This is a measure of the dispersion of a set of observations. If a large proportion of the observations cluster within a narrow range of values, there is less variability in the distribution than would be the case when there is a higher proportion of extreme values. Often-seen measures of variability in a distribution of observations are the standard deviation and standard error. A smaller standard deviation indicates greater precision of the value being estimated. Again, knowing precise statistical definitions and computational formulas is less important to understanding sabermetrics than is a comfort level with the concept.

Adjustment

The concept of adjustment appears often in sabermetric analysis. The rationale for adjusting is to increase comparability, to account for external factors that may confound associations. Perhaps the clearest example of the value of adjustment is in "park factors." The entry of mile-high Colorado into the major leagues has made it clear that ballparks can appreciably affect the balance between offense and defense. Whether intuitively or empirically, nearly everyone park-adjusts observed data from known hitters' or pitchers' parks. The process might be likened to adjusting for cost-of-living differences between, say, San Francisco and St. Louis. Similarly, most sabermetricians apply adjustments for time, seeking to improve comparability between, for example, the deadball era and the rabbit-ball era of the 1930s, or between the low-offense 1960s and today. This adjustment for era is analogous to the familiar adjustment for inflation in financial reporting, wherein prices are expressed in constant "1970 dollars."

Many types of adjustments are used by sabermetricians. For instance, after adjusting for park, year, level, and league, Clay Davenport standardizes the "average" season line to .270/.340/.430 (BA/OBP/SP) and .260 Equivalent Average when he calculates his Davenport Translations of major and minor league players. A researcher might adjust runs-based or wins-based season totals for players so that the sum of all individual players on a team equaled the team's total.

Weighting

Looking at sabermetric equations, you may be put off by the multipliers or coefficients you see. Multiply singles by 0.47? Subtract 0.60 the number of times caught stealing? These weightings arise from the researcher's analysis of the data. It's clear that hitting a single increases the likelihood of scoring, but scoring is by no means a certainty. Therefore, the coefficient for singles should lie somewhere between zero (no effect on run-scoring) and one (add a single, add a run). The reasoning for the negative effect of caught-stealing is similar, noting also that the damage to the offense from being caught stealing is greater than the boost from hitting a single. The reason, of course, is that in addition to removing a runner from the bases, the CS consumes a precious out.

What may make you uncomfortable about these sabermetric weightings is that they aren't necessarily integers. In truth, though, every baseball statistical formula uses weighted coefficients. For example, slugging percentage is (1 times singles, plus 2 times doubles, plus 3 times triples, plus 4 times homers) divided by (1 times at-bats). With a small change in weights—extra-base hits are all weighted as 1 instead of 2, 3, and 4—we calculate batting average. The weights used in traditional stats were not devised for empirical analysis and model-building. Sabermetric stats, driven by and calculated from large sets of observational data, look much messier than the traditional ones, but they are appreciably more powerful.

THE SABERMETRIC LITERATURE

As with research of any sort, a key part of preparing to do sabermetrics is to find out how other researchers have addressed the issues you've set out to study. The literature of sabermetrics appears in a variety of media, examples of which are discussed below. Before beginning, however, I must offer a disclaimer. As you'll see, much of the literature of sabermetrics is in computer sources instead of ink on paper. As Ted Hathaway mentioned *by Lyle Spatz / Chair, Baseball Records Committee*

The Baseball Records Committee is concerned with major league records of two specific types. One type of "record" has to do generally with superlative achievements by an individual, a team, or a league. These records can delineate any span of time. For example, Hank Aaron has the career record for most total bases (6,856), while pitcher Merle (Doc) Adkins holds the American League record for the most hits allowed in an inning (12). We also use the word "record" to refer to an individual player's game-by-game, season-by-season, or lifetime accomplishments. Clyde Passeau, for example, has a lifetime won-lost record of 162-150; in the 1947 season Brooklyn's Pete Reiser had 23 doubles; and on August 6, 1949, the Browns' Bob Dillinger had three hits in five times at bat.

The various repositories of records data are run by extremely knowledgeable people, and all are ready to make changes when researchers can prove to their satisfaction that something is in error. So whether you set out to research a particular record, or whether you stumble onto something new or that just doesn't seem right, you must provide proof to substantiate your claim.

Old newspapers are a wonderful source of information, but finding a single reference in a newspaper is usually not enough to make a case for change. For instance, Hall Lee of the Boston Braves had 422 at-bats in 1935 without hitting a home run. Now suppose you run across a Chicago newspaper from 1935 that says Lee hit an inside-the-park home run in the previous day's game at Braves Field. Don't immediately assume you've made a startling discovery and that the record books are wrong. Start checking the other Chicago newspapers and, even more important, in Boston, where the game was played. If all say Lee had a home run, then check the papers for the next week or so to make sure what they originally called a home run was not later changed to a triple and a throwing error.

Remember that baseball's "bookkeeping" has not always been as detailed and conscientious as it is today. Score books and the official day-by-day sheets from the game's early years are replete with omissions, transpositions, double-counting, addition errors, and what can best be described as illegibility. These errors occurred either in the accounting of individual games, or in the league's accounting at the end of the season. Moreover, for much of this early period, individual totals and league totals were not necessarily compared to see that they balanced.

"Official sheets" date from 1903 for the National League and from 1905 for the American League. Of course, not all statistical categories were kept in those early years. Runs batted in, earned run averages, batter strikeouts, batter hit-by-pitch, wild pitches, and passed balls are just some examples of statistical categories that began to be compiled at later dates.

Not everyone enjoys sitting in libraries, poring over microfilm of old newspapers and guides. Those who do, however, find it not only personally rewarding, they also know they've contributed to making the game's historical record more accurate.

in Chapter 4, these sources are a moving target in terms of both the content of what is available and the location of the materials. The Web site addresses of suggested readings and source materials are accurate as of the moment they are placed in this chapter, but there is no guarantee that that's where they will be when you read this. Similarly, materials appear on (and disappear from) the World Wide Web every day. The sources listed here should be taken as a selected snapshot of what's out there at this moment.

The universe of sabermetric literature can be divided into the four broad categories—books, printed annuals, scholarly journals, and online resources. This is by no means an exhaustive review of the available materials. It should be taken instead as a brief guide to the literature of sabermetrics.

Books

The nearest thing to a bible of sabermetrics is John Thorn and Pete Palmer's 1984 book *The Hidden Game of Baseball*, which thoroughly reviews the history of baseball statistics as of the mid-1980s, before laying out the basis for Palmer's Linear Weights methodology. Though long out of print, the book can be found in many libraries. Sabermetricians eagerly await Palmer's revision of the book, possibly to be published in 2001. The encyclopedic *Total Baseball*, now in its sixth edition, contains short essays on the historical development of baseball statistics and sabermetrics. Edited by Thorn, Palmer, and colleagues, those essays can be seen as highly condensed and updated portions of *The Hidden Game of Baseball*.

The prolific Bill James has crafted many books about the game. His sabermetric magnum opus is 1985's *Bill James Historical Baseball Abstract*, which extends the approach developed through his series of annual *Baseball Abstracts* to the full sweep of over a century of baseball, decade by decade from the 1870s through the 1980s. James is not really a statistical methodologist. Rather, he is a brilliant writer, critical thinker, and poser of intriguing and far-reaching questions about baseball.

In addition to the two giants of sabermetrics, you might also look at Craig Wright and Tom House's *The Diamond Appraised*, another out-of-print volume, from 1989. Michael Schell's 1999 *Baseball's All-Time Best Hitters*, while misleadingly titled (since most of the book discusses batting averages, which are far from a measure of the "best" hitting), is very sound methodologically and written in a clear and entertaining fashion. Although, in contrast to the other authors discussed in this section, Schell is a professor of biostatistics, his book contains few equations, little jargon, and no Greek symbols.

Printed Annuals

The model for sabermetric annuals is the *Bill James Baseball Abstract*. James self-published his work for several years before the first mass-market Ballantine edition of 1982. He ended the series with the 1988 edition.

At least three competitors vie for the niche opened by the *James Baseball Abstract*, still following the general plan he developed two decades ago. The annuals all contain essays reviewing each major league team's prior season, often with small statistical tidbits inserted to amplify and support the writer's point of view. They also offer commentaries, often entertainingly ironic or sarcastic, statistical profiles, and projections on current and future major league players, as well as longer essays on broader sabermetric subjects. The great majority of editors and contributors to the annuals are members of SABR. The three major competitors are:

- *Bill James Presents STATS Major League Handbook*, 2000 edition edited by John Dewan, Don Zminda, and colleagues—the most analytic volume in STATS Inc.'s extensive series of statistical breakdowns.
- *The Baseball Prospectus*, 2000 edition edited by Clay Davenport, Chris Kahrl, Joe Sheehan, and colleagues—featuring Davenport's Equivalent Runs approach, Michael Wolverton's Support-Neutral Win-Loss analysis, Rany Jazayerli's Pitcher Abuse Points, Davenport's "Wilton" forecasting system, and more.
- *The Big Bad Baseball Annual*, 2000 edition edited by Don Malcolm, Brock Hanke, Jim Furtado, and colleagues—including Furtado's Extrapolated Runs, Tom Ruane's Value Added approach, Malcolm's Quality Matrix, and more.

Scholarly Journals

Many baseball-based papers written in research journals are at least as interested in applying sophisticated analytic techniques to a dataset as they are with deriving results of great value in the game of baseball. These are, after all, serious academic journals. The equations and mathematical symbols are often quite daunting to even the most ardent of (nonstatistician) sabermetricians. Even so, a number of scholarly journals publish papers with baseball themes.

The American Statistical Association produces a range of journals, many of which have published at least a few baseball articles within the last several years. They range from the "popular" level *Chance*, through the "informal" *American Statistician*, to its flagship *Journal of the American Statistical Association*. For example, Jay Bennett's oft-mentioned 1993 article on Joe Jackson's performance in the 1919 World Series was published in *The American Statistician*. A more technical recent paper (by S.M. Berry, C.S. Reese, and P.D. Larkey, "Bridging different eras in sports," JASA 1999;94:661-676), describes the process of constructing statistical models for comparing players across time, in professional hockey and golf as well as baseball. Two of three commentaries published with the Berry paper were written by statistician-SABR members Jim Albert and Michael Schell.

In addition to the ASA journals, one might search for scholarly articles on baseball statistical topics in such journals as *Applied Statistics* and *Operations Research*. Along with the Web sites discussed below, ASA's Section on Statistics in Sports may be a useful place to start searching for references to such papers (www.amstat.org/sections/SIS/). Although it has not been updated since 1995, Charlie Pavitt's Statistical Baseball Research Bibliography (www.udel.edu/johnc/faculty/pavitt.html) is a useful resource for categorized references to both scholarly journals and sabermetric publications, including *By the Numbers*, the SABR Statistical Analysis Committee newsletter.

Online Resources

Although most of the major sabermetric books were written in the 1980s and have gone out of print, sabermetrics didn't stop a decade or two ago. Instead, it went electronic. Throughout the 1990s and continuing into today, sabermetricians have exchanged ideas and thoughts by email, by Internet, by Usenet, and on the Web.

In the early and mid-1990s, most of the best online sabermetric action took place in the Usenet newsgroup rec.sport.baseball and its subgroup rec.sport.baseball.analysis. Sadly, like much of Usenet, those newsgroups have long since degenerated into flamewars and woofs, with little content.

Email list-servers were the state of the art in the late 1980s and early 1990s, then fell by the wayside with the spread of the Web. More secure and more controllable than newsgroups, they seem to be making something of a comeback as the millennium turns. Although the mix of topics and threads on SABR's own email list, SABR-L (sabr-l@apple.ease.lsoft.com), is never static, sabermetric issues are often a significant part of the interchange. Many of the sabermetric Web sites listed below feature associated email lists and/or chat capability for people who register with the site, in addition to links pointing to other baseball discussions. Another email list where discussion of sabermetric issues is always welcome is my own STATLG-L, the "Baseball (and lesser sports) discussion list" (statlg-l@listserv.brown.edu).

It is all but impossible to catalog the breadth of sabermetric work available on the World Wide Web. As with so many other subject areas, the immense data storage capacity, ever-widening bandwidth, and rapidly increasing availability and acceptance of the Web have fostered an explosion of sabermetric information sources on the Web. What follows, then, is just a glance at what's out there waiting to be seen. Because the Web is built on hyperlinks, starting almost anywhere among the Web sites mentioned below will lead you to other sites (and other sites, and other sites, and ...) that you may find valuable.

- **John Skilton's Baseball Links**. The place to start any search for baseball information on the Web. In particular, check the section on "Stats & Analysis." www.baseball-links.com/links/Statistics_&_Analysis/)
- **Greg Spira's Baseball Pages**. Another excellent starting point. (www.baseballpages.com/)

- **SABR members' Web sites.** In particular, the annotated listing of sites devoted to baseball research and analysis. (www.sabr.org/research-links.shtml)
- **Baseball Prospectus Online.** (www.baseballprospectus.com/)
- **Big Bad Baseball.** (www.bigbadbaseball.com/)
- **The Baseball Archive.** Downloadable statistical database and more, including Grabiner's Sabermetric Manifesto, run by Sean Lahman. (www.baseball1.com/)
- **Stathead Consulting.** (www.stathead.com/): Keith Woolner operates this site.
- **Jim Furtado's Baseball Stuff.** (www.baseballstuff.com/mainindex/shtml) Partially associated with the Big Bad Baseball group, also hosts a variety of "baseball scholars.
- **Statistical Studies of Baseball.** Analyses by math professor John Jarvis. (pacer1.usca.sc.edu/~jfj/baseball.html)

Analytic Datasets

Just a few years ago—or, in terms of computational power and availability of information, many generations ago—obtaining data for a statistical analysis of baseball data meant copying down rows and columns of numbers from the Macmillan *Baseball Encyclopedia* or Sporting News publications such as the annual *Official Baseball Register* or *Baseball Guide,* or possibly Neft and Cohen's *Sports Encyclopedia: Baseball.* This was a mind-numbing and laborious task, fraught with the potential for transcription errors of all sorts. No wonder hardly anyone tried to do it!

Beginning in the 1980s, though, the dual thrusts of burgeoning interest in baseball and the rise of personal computers combined to fuel an explosion in baseball data availability. The data sources have expanded enormously in recent years, with more of the same on the horizon. In addition, highly detailed records of baseball events now coming on line present challenges and opportunities to sabermetric researchers.

Hard Copy

The day of the massive encyclopedia has not yet passed. The mantle of "official" encyclopedia has passed from the Macmillan volume to *Total Baseball,* now in its sixth edition. Every player in major league history is listed with his season-by-season numbers. For each league season, there are team stats (traditional and sabermetric) as well as leader boards for a variety of player stats. Many essays paint broad pictures of aspects of the game. The essays on the history of stats and on sabermetrics are fine background reading on the subject. The Neft and Cohen *Sports Encyclopedia: Baseball* is packed with seasonal totals and traditional stats, organized around team rosters year by year rather than a player-by-player career display. Both books remain useful as a means of wandering through the data, stopping whenever something catches your eye and prompts a question or thought to be explored more systematically using other sources of data.

If, for some reason, you're looking for situational stats, the various annual books from STATS Inc. offer them in every imaginable category.

CD-ROM

Several years ago, a number of CD-ROM baseball encyclopedias were on the market. Microsoft published a multimedia CD-ROM, heavier on video clips and sound files than on accessibility of the encyclopedia data, and an early edition of *Total Baseball* came with a CD-ROM version of the book. As with Microsoft's CD, search and download for analytic purposes took a backseat to multimedia and production values.

In any case, neither of those CD-ROMs lasted very long. At the time of this writing, the only commercial CD-ROM source of baseball statistics that I'm aware of is the *FanPark Baseball Encyclopedia*, produced by Miller Associates, also the authors of APBA's *Broadcast Blast* simulation game. Using datasets obtained from STATS Inc., the *Fanpark* encyclopedia contains team and player-season data (both traditional and sabermetric) on batting, pitching, and fielding, beginning with the 1876 National League and continuing to the present day with annual updates. A built-in query engine permits a range of queries using such criteria as years, leagues, positions, and batting or throwing side. For example, you could construct a leader board of, say, the top ten career slugging percentages for left-handed-hitting middle infielders since the end of World War II. (If you must know, Joe Morgan tops the list at .427, with Lou Whitaker right behind at .426.) If you have a query not covered by the internal engine, however, you're out of luck. Another shortcoming of the *FanPark* encyclopedia from the sabermetrician's viewpoint is that data from the CD cannot be exported to a spreadsheet or other analytic software for further analysis.

Online Datasets

One of the most valuable resources for sabermetricians is the increasing availability of baseball datasets on the World Wide Web. Although some such datasets demand payment, some of the very best and most extensive ask nothing more of the requester than his or her name and email address.

At this time, the most complete database of baseball data on the Web is supplied by SABR member Sean Lahman at his site called **The Baseball Archive**, at the URL (www.baseball1.com). The database covers the entire existence of major league baseball, as far back as the National Association in 1871 and as recent as 1999. In its native format of Microsoft Access97, there are separate tables of player-season totals (regular season and postseason) for batting, pitching, and fielding. In addition, Lahman has built tables of all teams' seasonal records, players who've participated in All-Star games, the Hall of Fame, and managers. All player tables are linked by the unique "player ID" field, leading to a master table of birth date, batting side, throwing arm, and debut-year information on each of the 15,351 men who had played or managed in the big leagues through 1999.

The MS Access database can be downloaded as a self-extracting ZIP file from Lahman's Web site. This 6 MB file unzips to the full database that occupies approximately 16 MB of your hard drive. If you don't use MS Access, a comma-delimited flat-file version of the database tables is in a 4 MB self-extracting ZIP file. The flat-file can be imported into almost any database or spreadsheet of your choice, if the application can accept files as large as these; the batting table contains nearly 80,000 records.

Programmer Sean Forman has written an extensive Web application for the **Big Bad Baseball** Web site that offers a quick look at the breadth of the information contained in the Lahman database. Located at www.bigbadbaseball.com/stats/, it has hyperlinks connecting innumerable fields. You might start out looking at Richie Ashburn's career and note that the most similar player to Ashburn is Brett Butler. Click on Butler and you might want to see the roster of his 1987 Indians, who finished seventh in the AL East that year. One more click, and you can get the standings and team stats for the entire league that season. Or you could look at the managerial records of Pat Corrales, fired during the season, and Doc Edwards. Or Sammy Stewart's pitching numbers. Clicking on Stewart, we see that the most similar pitcher is Tom Sturdivant. Who might lead you to the Yankees of the late 1950s or the 1964 Kansas City A's. And on and on and on and....
Although other statistical datasets exist on the Web, as far as I know Lahman's is the only all-season one available without cost for download and analysis. Data on individual players through 1998 can be viewed at the **Total Baseball** site (www.totalbaseball.com/), but nothing is downloadable. During the baseball season, the Web site of **Major League Baseball** (www.majorleaguebaseball.com/u/baseball/mlb/stats.htm) updates current season player totals daily. These tabular reports are sortable) but not easily downloadable.

On an entirely different level of data, play-by-play event data on a number of seasons are downloadable from **Retrosheet** (www.retrosheet.org/index.html). This volunteer organization, founded by David Smith in 1989, is dedicated to the goal of finding score-sheets, newspaper accounts, or any other play-by-play records of every game played in the history of major league baseball. These accounts are rescored using a standardized and highly detailed scoring system, and then entered into computer files. Further computer processing creates "event files" of every play of every game, in a format that can be imported into spreadsheet or database programs for analysis. The basic outline of the Retrosheet scoring system originated in Project Scoresheet, another product of the fertile mind of Bill James, which started scoring games in the 1984 season. At this writing, the Retrosheet Web site offers for download 21 complete league-season datasets, both leagues for each year between 1980 and 1989, plus the 1967 American League. The 1984-1989 files are actually the property of Total Sports Inc., the custodian of all Project Scoresheet data through 1998. Retrosheet also offers several programs specifically designed to aid in working with their datasets, including one that will prepare the flat-file datasets for import into database or spreadsheet applications.

STATE OF THE ART

Sabermetric research has been more successful in some areas than others. In large part, useful sabermetric research is a function of the richness and fullness of the data being studied. It should come as no surprise, then, that offense is by far the most advanced area of research. Information is readily available on many forms of offensive success (the four types of hits, walks, steals, and such) and also on offensive failure (outs, double plays, caught stealing). Conversely, research into fielding has not yet obtained satisfying results.

In an essay in the 2000 edition of the *Baseball Prospectus*, Keith Woolner describes what he terms "Baseball's Hilbert Problems." Taking as his inspiration a speech in 1900 by mathematician David Hilbert outlining challenging research issues in mathematics for the upcoming century, Woolner suggests twenty-three topic areas where sabermetric research might venture in the near future.

Woolner's vision is extremely broad. He discusses topics ranging from the refinement of on-field performance evaluation to roster design to pitcher usage patterns to assessment of draft picks and trades, and much more. Whether sabermetrics is really the right toolkit to address these particular issues is an open question. Even if it turns out that sabermetric analytic techniques don't shed a great deal of light on the vexing problems Woolner describes, the search will undoubtedly open exciting new avenues for empirical investigation of baseball.

For those with an empirical bent, sabermetrics can enhance the experience of baseball. It adds to your appreciation of the skills displayed on the field, adds to your enjoyment in a pitchers' duel or in a slugfest, adds to your arguments about whether to steal or hit-and-run or bring in a lefty or make a double switch, adds to your sense of the sweeping and ever-changing history of the game. All in all, it adds a great deal to your total enjoyment of the beautiful game that is baseball.

The "search for objective knowledge" has permeated baseball from its earliest days, from Henry Chadwick through Branch Rickey and Allan Roth, and beyond. In the 1980s, Bill James played a leading role in popularizing empirical examination of large-scale datasets. As computing power became more available and easier to use, more people were empowered to study the data and to address an ever wider variety of questions about the game. Sabermetrics offers the opportunity for sharing, exchanging, critiquing, challenging, and further expanding research ideas. The research atmosphere is collegial and competitive, passionate and invigorating.

As a concluding thought, I offer an aphorism that can be taken as a challenge or as a caution to sabermetrician and non-sabermetrician alike. Though often credited to Albert Einstein, at least one source indicates that it originated with an English medical researcher, Sir George Pickering, and was often quoted by Einstein: "Not everything that can be counted counts, and not everything that counts can be counted."

Chapter Six

CHECKING THE FACTS
by Cappy Gagnon

Before I had ever done any serious baseball research, I had acquired a college degree in journalism, done graduate work in English, and taught high school English for four years. I had also edited several training publications and had even been published in *Baseball Digest*. Useful as those experiences were in teaching me how to research a subject, they pale in comparison to what I learned about fact checking during the next two decades in my main area of employment—law enforcement.

The knowledge I'm referring to is not just a cop's compassionate response to persons who have suffered at the hands of those with too many human frailties. No, I'm referring to the wisdom that all cops acquire—wisdom directly applicable, it seems to me, to checking the accuracy of sources in baseball research.

Skepticism and Doggedness

That's what you need. Skepticism and doggedness. Nothing more. Don't believe everything you hear or read, and don't give up. Don't leave any stone unturned. Keep checking, rechecking, disbelieving, and verifying. Police officers are taught to listen and observe very carefully when interviewing victims, witnesses, complainants, and suspects. What they are taught, you should apply. You should...

- ✆ accurately record the information you receive
- ✆ ask questions to clarify what you have learned
- ✆ probe the answers you get to make sure the information is unbiased, truthful, and fully disclosed.

Of course, skepticism can lead to cynicism. Police training, coupled with the human condition, sometimes causes well-meaning law enforcement officers to become embittered. But a healthy amount of skepticism can be useful. It has helped me plow though much baseball information to determine what is wheat and what is chaff.

To take an example: In my continuing research on Notre Dame men who played major league baseball, I have come across many frustrating false leads. Imagine my joy when I read in an early 1930s *Who's Who in Baseball* that Zeke Bonura, a star first baseman in both the majors and minors, had attended Notre Dame. Moreover, no less an icon than Knute Rockne had given Bonura his nickname ("Zeke" being short for physique, since Bonura, a star high school javelin thrower, had a strong, athletic body). Why hadn't I known that Bonura was a Notre Dame man? Skepticism crept in. I hadn't known it because it wasn't true. *Who's Who* had gotten it wrong. While Rockne may have given Zeke his nickname, he didn't do so at Notre Dame. It may have happened on one of Rockne's high school recruiting trips. I just don't know.

Doggedness is as important as skepticism. A good baseball researcher—like a good police detective—has to be persistent. Every lead that is uncovered must be examined, followed up, studied, evaluated, and, only then, either embraced or discarded.

Dick Thompson, who would have to be an "original inductee" into the SABR Fact Checking Hall of Fame, is a firm believer in persistence. When he and I went through 120 shoeboxes full of notes from the late Tom Shea, we found a reference indicating that Les Mann, a journeyman outfielder in the 1910s and '20s, had attended Springfield College. Over the next decade I sent four different letters to the archivist at the college, asking about Mann. Each letter was answered with "no record found." Both Dick and I believed in the scrupulousness of Tom Shea's research (our skepticism being aimed more at the archivist). I sent another letter. On the fifth try, I learned that Les Mann was indeed a graduate of Springfield College and was one of the great athletes in the history of the school. I also received a detailed chronology of his life.

Be dogged. Trust your best sources—but verify them conclusively if you can.

Be a Fan, but Know Your Facts

Baseball occupies a unique place among all sports when it comes to embracing its history and lore. As a game with just the right amount of pacing to permit discussion—between pitches, innings, relief changes, pinch hitters, etc., and in barber shops, taverns, and across backyard fences—baseball, like no other sport, inspires arguments over strategy and the relative merits of teams and players. Fans and researchers can argue forever over which is the best baseball book. Can anyone even name more than a couple of good books about football, basketball, or hockey? As for movies: For every *Hoosiers* or *Rudy*, there are dozens of fine films about baseball.

One reason baseball keeps thriving as a "hot stove" topic is that it has a body of research that can be examined, massaged, reinvigorated, and—occasionally—corrected. The Society for American Baseball Research, spearheaded by Bob Davids, Pete Palmer, Bill James, and many others, has led the way in making baseball a subject of serious research. While baseball discussions will always be tinged with partisanship, it's heartening when the disputants know the facts about the game—when they can separate history from lore. Even these debates benefit from precision about the facts.

Fact checking and a commitment to accuracy are essential ingredients in baseball research. In 1977 Bob Davids, founder of SABR, took me on my first trip to the Library of Congress. I came away with several useful reminders for anyone who aspires to do research on the National Pastime. Here are a few:

All Sources Are Useful

I once asked a newspaperman about a book he had written about a player who had just finished a fine rookie season. He shook his head. "It's a book I wouldn't read," he said. Clearly, he didn't think what he had written was worthwhile. Viewing his remark from the perspective of a researcher, I disagree. Even his hasty, superficial tome has potential value. When researching a topic, you will want to read everything you can get your hands on concerning it. Even the dross may contain a nugget of gold. This helps you to...

Develop Many Leads

While researching a subject, you will want to glean as many facts as you can. If you're doing biographical research on a ballplayer, you'll want to know the following:

- ❷ Where was the player born?
- ❷ Who were his parents?
- ❷ Where did he grow up?
- ❷ Where did he go to school?
- ❷ For what teams did he play while an amateur?
- ❷ When did he first turn professional?
- ❷ For which pro teams did he play?
- ❷ What persons have first-hand knowledge about his life and career?

Don't accept a single source as the final answer to any of these questions. Keep looking. Whenever you find a second or third answer to the same question, you're doing fact checking, even if you don't think about it that way. It's possible, of course, that all the writers you've read have relied on the same source, in which case your cross-checking has proved nothing. It has merely shown that writers rely on one another, sometimes too heavily. Or, if you're a cynic, it has proved that...

Not Everything in Print Is Accurate

Nor is everything necessarily accurate on the Internet either, as you probably realize. Jack Tackach, in his article "Hazards and Tips for Researchers" in the 1986 *Baseball Research Journal*, tells how he went about assessing the validity of three conflicting versions of the suspension of pitcher Charles Sweeney from the Providence Grays in July 1884. Nineteenth-century baseball reporting abounds in disparate accounts of the same event. The same challenge of differing reportage is with us today, although modern baseball writers, in general, take their task more seriously than did the journalists of the 1880s.

What Tackach did in researching Charles "Old Hoss" Radbourn and the Providence team for his New York *Times* article, including how he resolved the Sweeney question, is a case study in fact checking. The author concludes his article with four strategies and tips. Here they are, although without Tackach's explanation of each one:

1. Trust primary sources rather than secondary sources.
2. Mistrust books written by ballplayers, even if they are primary sources.
3. When faced with several versions of the same story, accept the version that acknowledges sources and shows an awareness of conflicting views.
4. For statistics, use *The Baseball Encyclopedia*, published by Macmillan. (Times change. Better make that *Total Baseball*, published by Total Sports, since the 10th edition [1996] of Macmillan's classic reference was its last from that publisher.)

Repetition Does Not Prove Accuracy

My research led me to the life and career of Louis "Chief" Sockalexis. I came across several references to his having raised his batting average to well over .400 late into his 1897 rookie season, before tailing off to his eventual .338 mark. That seemed like a precipitous drop. I was curious about how the great Cleveland Spiders' outfielder could have put together so many 0-fers. I decided to track his season batting average from opening day as it rose and fell. Guess what? The .400 average didn't happen. It was a typo. An oft-repeated typo, but nothing more than a goof of the Linotype operator. (A note for younger readers: In the old days, a Linotype operator did what today would be called keyboarding, but he—always he—did it with hot metal type on a machine the size of a mainframe.)

Not All Primary Sources Are Reliable

Now, here's a problem. Even though primary sources—words straight from the horse's mouth—are likely to be more accurate than secondary sources, they aren't gospel. A filled-in scorecard from a baseball game you saw years ago is a primary source. It should be correct, but it may not be. A newspaper box score is usually regarded as a primary source, although technically the official scorer's score-sheet, which the newspaper's box score is assumed to match, is the primary source. Another primary source is a player's completed questionnaire at the National Baseball Library. But be careful. I have seen some erroneous facts in the players' own handwriting on questionnaires they have filled out for the SABR/Hall of Fame Biographical Research Project. Some of these errors are

by Bob McConnell / Chair, Minor League Committee

Minor league research can cover a wide range of topics. The three most common topics are club and league histories, compilation of batting and pitching statistics for leagues where these stats have never been published, and putting together player career records.

The Baseball Hall of Fame Library is a great source of information. It has a large collection of record books, yearbooks, and media guides. It also has a complete set of annual guides and microfilm of several weekly baseball newspapers. The library has a file for every player who ever played in the majors, and there is a great deal of minor league information in these files. For a researcher working on career records, there is a National Association contract record file. This card file lists all legal transactions, such as contract signings, sales, releases, suspensions, etc. The library also has an extensive file of photographs.

The Sporting News office in St. Louis has a somewhat similar research facility. It has player card files for thousands of minor league players, a complete set of annual guides, a complete run of *The Sporting News* on microfilm, and a photographic file of over 600,000 images.

When it gets down to real original research, old newspapers are the primary source. The Library of Congress in Washington has a fabulous collection of newspapers on microfilm. The library participates in Interlibrary Loan. In Chapter 2, "Introduction to Libraries and Archives," Steve Gietschier explains in detail the use of the Interlibrary Loan system.

The *SABR Guide to Minor League Statistics* lists, year by year, all of the minor league statistics that appeared in the various guides and weekly newspapers. If you want to find out if the *Spalding Guide* included RBIs in the Texas League averages for 1920, it's in the book. The book contains a supplement showing, on a year-by-year basis, the box scores of the minor leagues covered in *Sporting Life* and *The Sporting News*.

A very useful research tool is a year-by-year alphabetical list of every player included in the averages in the guide for that year. The player's league and batting average are given so that he can be easily found in the guide. SABR member Art Cantu has prepared this list, and you can obtain a copy from him.

The Encyclopedia of Minor League Baseball offers a wealth of information. It lists, on a year-by-year basis, all National Association leagues plus a few strong non-NA leagues. Included in the listing are the league president and league classification; club standings with club nicknames; W-L records, managers, and attendance (some pre-World War II and almost all post-World War II). It also gives batting and pitching leaders in the main categories, outstanding events of the year, and farm system affiliations. The second edition of the *Encyclopedia* came out in 1997, and another edition is planned.

omissions. Some may have resulted from a failing memory because of the passage of time. Others may be shadings of the truth to highlight the best and downplay the worst. Be skeptical, as always.

Not All Secondary Sources Are Unreliable

This point relates to my advice to read as much as you can. As stories pass from one teller to the next, they often lose clarity. Try playing "Pass It Along" if you don't believe me. But sometimes even Bill Stern-type history can be used to backtrack and locate kernels of truth. Remember that while plenty of slapdash baseball books have been published over the years, many excellent and reliable ones have been published, too, as Andy McCue makes clear in Chapter 3. A good secondary source can be an ideal starting point for research, particularly if it contains a bibliography and/or source notes. The better the secondary source, the more valuable it is as a fact-checking tool.

Three Criteria for Judging Sources

Common sense is indispensable to a researcher. The old saying applies: "If it sounds too good to be true, it probably is." I was skeptical about Lou Sockalexis's flirting with a .400 batting mark in his rookie year, and my skepticism was justified. SABR researcher David Kemp wondered in the early 1980s whether Walter Malmquist had really batted .477 for York in the Nebraska State League in 1913, as the *Reach Guide* showed. That towering .477 gave Malmquist the highest season batting average in minor league history. Kemp decided to check. Through a box-score search in the York and Grand Island, Nebraska, newspapers, he determined that .477 was almost certainly not correct. Incomplete box scores gave Malmquist only a .342 percentage. Kemp's skepticism and fact checking erased the York hitter from the record books. The record holder became Gary Redus, who in 1978 batted. .462 for Billings, Montana, in the short-season Pioneer League (according to *The Encyclopedia of Minor League Baseball*).

In *The Baseball Research Handbook*, Jerry Tomlinson listed three criteria for judging the accuracy of sources. They sum up much of what I've said in this chapter. They are:

- **Proximity.** A newspaper reporter commenting on a play he observed that very day is likely to be more reliable than a writer interpreting the play fifty years later. The reporter had the considerable advantage of closeness in time and space.

- **Competence.** Some reporters are more skilled than others. Some historians are more capable and conscientious than others. Writers don't carry around gold badges proclaiming their competence, but time and thought should enable you to reach your own conclusions as to who is trustworthy and who isn't.

❶ Objectivity. A person with an ax to grind is not an ideal source. What you want is a source that has nothing to gain or lose by telling the truth. A lack of objectivity can affect autobiographies ("What will my grandchildren think?") and can also taint biographies ("I'd better jazz this up a bit.").

Record All Your Notes Clearly

There is nothing more embarrassing than to go back to your notes after an interview or after having strained your eyes on microfilm of a long defunct newspaper—and then to be unable to read what you've written. I speak from experience. Make photocopies. Or print slowly and distinctly. Or take along your laptop. Don't be put in the position of having to telephone your interviewee in Caracas or return in person to Distant City, Illinois, to recheck facts that you should already have…that you do already have…but can't decipher.

Admit Your Mistakes

In compiling an all-Fighting-Irish baseball team, I put Roger Bresnahan, "The Duke of Tralee," behind the plate. I thought I had a great source for it. Bresnahan is listed in a publication dated 1916 as a Notre Dame letter winner. It seemed to me that 1916 was contemporaneous enough to be accurate. Bresnahan played for the Cubs in 1915, his last major league season. I had a legitimate-looking source, but it was wrong. The Hall of Fame catcher never attended Notre Dame.

Did Bresnahan simply make up his affiliation with the Fighting Irish? Perhaps. He also apparently convinced at least one writer that he had been born in Ireland, instead of in Toledo, Ohio. I take some comfort in knowing that I was not the only one fooled by his probably good-natured blarney.

I was also pleased to learn that Con Lucid, a so-so nineteenth-century pitcher who really was born in Ireland, claimed to be a Notre Dame man. Or at least his obituary did. The obit from a Houston newspaper in 1931 was as complete and glowing a biography as I have ever read. Some of the minor factual details argued strongly for its authenticity. But the obituary, charming as it was, proved to be anything but an accurate account of the life and career of Con Lucid. It was, in a word, fiction. Scratch another name from the Notre Dame roster.

No matter how careful you are, you, too, will make mistakes like this. It's embarrassing, but it can help other researchers. The readers of this chapter now know, for instance, that Roger Bresnahan and Con Lucid did not—repeat did not—attend Notre Dame.

…and Babe Ruth Had a Finite Number of Roommates

As a final note, my mother sends me obituaries from the Boston newspapers whenever a former major league ballplayer passes away. As least two of these men are described as "Babe Ruth's roommate." Long-time SABR member Bob Hoie, a first-ballot Hall of Fame fact checker, confirms that these two never got closer to Babe Ruth's hotel room than the Babe himself did on most nights.

Skepticism and doggedness. Apply them liberally, and you can't go wrong. Well, you can go wrong, but one or more hawkeyed SABR readers will probably let you know if you do.

Chapter Seven

FINDING AND USING PICTURES
by Mark Rucker

Pictures are an integral part of most baseball books, magazines, and monographs. They usually provide visual context for the places, people, and events described in the text. But what many do not understand is that pictures can guide a story, can establish the context for a thesis, or create a story themselves, connected through running captions. Images are most often used to elaborate or add to a text. The old saw about a picture being worth a thousand words is often true. With judicious imagery a story can be both more appealing and of more use to future researchers. And through visual imagery some of the best stories can be told, using very few words.

When determining the need for illustrations, authors often disagree with publishers. Many times publishers will insert a useless and ugly signature of photos that does very little to enhance the text. Authors seem to prefer imagery that accompanies the textual reference and is placed throughout the volume, even though picture quality may be sacrificed to bad paper. In any case, publishers have determined that book buyers expect pictures. In many situations, groups of images, organized in any number of ways, can bring a topic into focus. The more creative the use of imagery, the greater the chance of conveying visual information effectively, especially when pictures are set up to communicate one to another. A small number of pictures well placed will do more for the reader than a sheaf of overused, poorly printed or arranged photos ganged up in the middle of a book.

The complications of the search for pictures will be determined by the number of images needed and their rarity. Let's explore three completely hypothetical situations, each an example of a different level of complexity.

An Easy Search

Say you need to come up with ten photos illustrating players discussed in the text. You may prefer action shots to portraits, or you may want only head shots. This task should be a fairly easy one, unless you are working with eras like the 1850s or late 1890s. The automatic call will go to the National Baseball Library in Cooperstown, or you may wish to try major agencies such as Corbis/Bettmann or AP/Wide World. There are also smaller agencies that specialize in baseball. One of them is Photo File. Another is Transcendental Graphics, which is operated by the author of this chapter.

A request for portraits to any of these companies will bring results, but prices will vary, and the freshness of the images will also vary. Some photo sources offer only photographs that have been published many times before, producing a predictable look. Getting a fresh image, one which is either unpublished or unusual for any number of reasons, is preferable when making your choices. Inventive approaches can lead to useful discoveries, or to dead ends. For example, if your ten photos are to be of Detroit Tigers' players, you might want to contact the Detroit Public Library, which holds two or three baseball photo collections. You may not find precisely what you need, but the search is worth your while. Historical societies and libraries in other major or minor league cities frequently yield interesting material. This kind of search, being rather simple, can be accomplished with a minimum of effort.

A Not-So-Easy Search

In this case your task is to find fifty to 100 photos to be placed throughout a 250-page book. You want to find images not only to fit with the text but also to illuminate some discoveries made in your research. This means, as your topic dictates, you must have photos of the St. Louis Browns wearing uniforms used only in the years 1904 to 1930. There are few written descriptions of some of these uniforms, but pictures proving the existence of a number of one-year designs help to distinguish photographs of different years. This ties in with your study of the athletic garment industry of the early twentieth century and with its connections to the main sporting goods companies then supplying the major leagues. In some years only certain manufacturers were hired. These manufacturers produced the home uniforms for the Browns, but not the road uniforms. Why they provided only home uniforms—the politics, the economics, the backroom deals—is the story you want to tell as you chronicle twenty-seven seasons with the Browns.

Huntin' and Whittlin'

First, get every pictorial book you can on the subject. For this assignment, you would look for books on the Browns, the AL in the early twentieth century, pictorial books on the industrial revolution in which textiles are well represented, and anything on sporting goods companies from the same era. When you see a picture you like, check its source in the photo credits of the book. Keep a running list of images you want and where they come from. If the books are old, the credits may be from companies no longer in business, and so old books list no credits at all. Making copies from old sources is always possible, but these decisions must be made on a case-by-case basis. If you see, for example, that *The Sporting News* (TSN) is a listed credit for a great Barney Pelty pitching shot, check with them. TSN has done an excellent job of maintaining files and providing them at reasonable rates. Then check the library for guides to historical societies, looking for Missouri listings, most likely in St. Louis or at the state capital in Jefferson City. Check the availability of pictorial archives in the St. Louis Public Library, and ask the archivists if they know other sources. Use each piece of information to lead to more information whenever you can.

If you want to end up with about seventy-five images in the book, try to get at least 200 possible pictures to choose from. The more you locate, the better the final selection—and the better the book—will be.

Ask for all pertinent materials from the picture agencies, libraries, and historical societies. They will usually be provided to you in the form of photocopies. Be sure to ask not just for photographs, because broadsides, advertisements, popular art, cartoons, pins, buttons, tickets, trading cards, scorecards, sheet music, ribbons, pennants, and banners can all be useful in making a visual statement. Sometimes these items turn up in collections other than baseball ones within repositories. It's always worth a question, because maybe a group of sports scrapbooks from eastern Missouri, let's say, was put together between 1903 and 1928 and is housed in the sociological collections. Or you may find that an entire shelf of materials from the textile mill you are studying does indeed reside in the Missouri Historical Society, but in their Kansas City branch.

Another worthwhile inquiry has to do with whether the collection contains original bound volumes of newspapers. These can be successfully photographed, if not too far decayed. Usually, the printouts from microfilm printers are too poor to use. Since you are dealing with many pictures on similar subjects, you must try to obtain not only a quantity of images but ones of high quality as well. Out-of-focus, overly dark or overly light pictures should be used only when desperately needed. Getting the critical mass of images together is the biggest job. So ask—and sometimes you will receive.

Next, you must make a series of cuts whereby the total number you have is whittled down to a publishable number. The pictures must be judged according to…

- ❶ direct importance to your text
- ❶ general historical importance
- ❶ image quality (which includes tones, density, and focus)
- ❶ visual impact (includes composition, cropping, and intensity)

In going through the group, there will always be images that you particularly like. Trust your judgment, because if you find them attractive, others will also. Since these pictures will be scattered through the book, one appearing perhaps on every three pages, they must be able to stand alone, requiring no other visual reference to be understood. They must read very clearly and be placed and sized for maximum impact. A portrait, for instance, is easy to work with, because the information it contains is simple. It can be easily read as a human form and can be included at almost any size, although huge is not usually a good idea. Conversely, a portrait can also be the dullest of all imagery, being static and predictable. When choosing an image with lots of information, you must plan to size it large enough to understand the detail. Where a head shot can be run very small, a shot of a sliding play at third base with a stadium crowd in the background cannot. This can lead to some frustration. Sometimes very fine pictures that work in every other way cannot be included because they do not read within the confines of a book page. Be willing to make some tough calls.

You must contact the agencies or other organizations that own the images and make arrangements for payment. Ideally, your publisher will perform this service for you. Often, however, you must do the job yourself under the looming cloud of an ungenerous budget. I cannot say much about prices, except that they vary greatly. The nicest thing about doing a book on the Browns is that you do not encounter copyright problems. Virtually everything you could find and would want to reproduce on this team is clearly in the public domain.

A Difficult Search

This time you are going to put together a picture book that includes at least 300 to 350 images over 180 pages. First, a few words about pictorial books are in order. It is most important that your subject be suitable. Jimmy Collins' life story may make an interesting read, but there is no way to find enough pictures to support a book. In the same way, a pictorial book on the Federal League would be difficult, and one on the nineteenth-century Union Association would be all but impossible. Safer territory includes team histories, picture bios of very famous players, and general histories of baseball. How many images do you need to proceed with your proposed book? Any topic for which 1,200+ fine pictures exist can be edited to yield 300 quite nicely. Then, out of these 300 a story must be told. Whether based on chronology (by decade or otherwise), or organized to emphasize certain images, events, or other aspects of the game, the selections should come from many excellent examples gathered from a variety of sources. In organizing the pictures, certain patterns will begin to appear—patterns and groupings that can be used to advantage in book design. The visual interplay of images is vital to the success of a pictorial, and this sometimes means that photo choices are guided by composition, not content.

Keeping many photos on the "possible" list is a good idea, perhaps up to 600 of them. You will probably have to request many more prints, transparencies, or scans than can be used in the book. This is just a cost of doing business in a project like this. But the use fees for these photos can be alarming, and this makes the acquisition of photos simultaneously an aesthetic, financial, and time-driven activity. The more suppliers you deal with, the wider the variety of quality, timeliness, and prices you will see.

RESEARCHING THE NEGRO LEAGUES

Dick Clark / Chair, Negro Leagues Committee, with Larry Lester and Patrick Rock

Robert Peterson in his landmark book, *Only the Ball Was White*, said, "Tracing the course of the organized Negro Leagues is rather like trying to follow a single black strand through a ton of spaghetti. The footing is infirm, and the strand has a tendency to break off in one's hand and slither back into the amorphous mass."

Researchers turning their attention to the Negro Leagues learn this quickly: Sources are often fragmentary, scattered, contradictory, or nonexistent. Most hometown newspapers did not report the results of road games. You must order microfilm of newspapers from other cities through Interlibrary Loan (ILL). Some newspapers are not available. Many issues even of major black weeklies were never archived, such as the 1919 Kansas City *Call* and the 1923 Indianapolis *Freeman*. Sometimes newspapers have no report of a game because it was played in a nearby town or in a non-league city. Sometimes papers reported only a line score, or just a few sentences confirming that the teams did play and giving the final score. In some mainstream white dailies, Negro League games were an afterthought, included as page fillers or buried under the heading "minor" or "amateur" baseball.

Even if you find a box score, it may lack important details: earned runs, strikeouts, walks, extra-base hits, stolen bases, RBIs, and individual runs scored. Sometimes you can generate the missing statistics from the accompanying text. The most difficult to recreate are at-bats, a common omission in Eastern newspapers. Box-score totals often do not sum correctly.

Midway through the season you will find teams disappearing from the news, only to discover the following year that they folded. One clue is the final standings, which show certain teams playing fewer games than the league leaders.

Come October, the most popular sport in the heyday of shadow ball was college football. You may find Jackie Robinson scoring touchdowns for UCLA, while the Homestead Grays are barely mentioned in winning their umpteenth league title. Even some Negro World Series games were not reported.

You will come across phantom players, resulting from misspelled names, names that were spelled phonetically, or even uneducated guesses "Rix" for "Ricks," "Early for Hurley," "Johnson" for "Johnston." An athlete may have played under a fictitious name to protect his college eligibility. In the early days, you will find box scores listing just the player's nickname, like "Geetchie" for Bluford Meredith, or "Cyclone Joe" for Smokey Joe Williams.

You have to make several decisions when compiling your data. Do you include games played against the teams of associated leagues? How about games played at neutral sites? Do you count as league games contests played in ballparks other than major league parks? It is fair to say that with the possible exception of researching baseball in the nineteenth century, the Negro Leagues remain the baseball researcher's most challenging task.

Casting a Wide Net

Ah, yes, the suppliers. For a project like this, no less than an all-out search will do. It will be necessary to make requests to every possible source, including all those mentioned above. Now, however, private collections should also be accessed wherever possible. But beware of the territory you are entering. Collectors can have absolutely fantastic material, key items that can sometimes make a book work. But the attitudes and requirements of collectors can create challenging situations. Many collectors want to share their materials, believing that sharing history is beneficial for all. But others fear the viewing of their holdings. They don't want the nature or contents of their collections to become public. I have even heard the amazing theory that original photos and original memorabilia will be devalued if reproduced in any publication. Reaching an agreement with a collector who owns important pictures for your project should be a top priority.

Let's say your book is to be a pictorial history of the Chicago White Sox. This project would require approaches to the Chicago Public Library, the Chicago Historical Society, the Chicago White Sox Baseball Club, the various agencies listed in the Chicago yellow pages under "Photographs—Stock," the owners of the largest card and memorabilia stores to inquire about local collectors who might be helpful, and any sports clubs or organizations, particularly on the South Side. A scheduled visit with George Brace, famous North Side photographer and archivist, would be a must. George, who knows more about Chicago baseball photography than anyone else, has thousands of pictures of the Sox. His files can almost always produce needed photos of very, very obscure players.

Still the hunt must go on. After checking with all the repositories already mentioned, you should expand your search far and wide, coast to coast, wherever your leads take you. It is important to remember that to get a group of 1,200 workable photos means that you will need to review probably four times that many. To search the largest public sources for imagery, which are in Washington, D.C., will require inquiries to the Library of Congress, mainly in their picture and photograph division, possibly in their film archive, and then on to the National Archives, where you will find possibly three or four collections that contain useful materials. The Illinois State Archives and State Library in Springfield might not only produce visual pieces but also open up some new leads in the southern part of the state. If you find other locations that may house such items as original old newspapers, a photo morgue from a Chicago paper, or files of importance from the team, make every effort to go visit.

And, for many, the first place to begin this whole process, now that our century starts with a crooked number, is in cyberspace. Don't forget to use the Internet.

Choices, Rights, and Costs

Once your gigantic stack of photocopies is spread out around your workplace, you will first want to determine that you have proper representation from decade to decade, with plenty of shots of players important to the team. You should have images in every possible genre, with photography predominating. To make a large book hold the interest of a viewer, you will want to pay particular attention to colorful small items that can be used to jazz up a spread or to add information to an adjacent photo. This means pins and buttons, ribbons and lapel ornaments, matchbook covers and ticket stubs, decals and ice cream lids, box tops and Sunday comics, postage stamps and cigar bands—all of which can be easily woven into the pattern of a visual story. These should accompany the display and magazine advertisements, program covers, score sheets, plastic cups, ballpark souvenirs, bubble gum cards, stereo views, magic lantern slides, toy pennants, panoramic team shots, vignettes from club collages, board game boxes, and newspaper banner headlines.

After your initial cuts are made, you must order actual reproductions. Then, with the 600 images in hand (your planned final total, remember, is 300 to 350), you will want to see how they look together. Did some of them actually look better as photocopies? The selection process can be complex and sometimes frustrating, but it can also be the most purely pleasing part of the process. But what is not so pleasant is the legal quagmire you wade into each time you publish even a fifty-year-old image.

When you deal with AP/Wide World or *The Sporting News* or Corbis/Bettmann, you are paying the rights holder directly. But when you deal with libraries and collections holding images from all kinds of creators, it becomes your problem to determine the copyright status of the image and, if necessary, to make proper payment. You may receive disclaimers, in legalese, from some sources. These documents should give you pause. The possibility of copyright infringement in a project this complicated is fairly high, unless you take proper precautions and know the law. Agencies and other sources can give you guidance about a picture with an unknown copyright status, but the ultimate responsibility is yours. Before paying rights-to-reproduce fees to anyone in a major project like this, I would strongly advise a visit to a copyright lawyer in order to understand exactly what is necessary to insure proper crediting and payment for all images. Take care of this early, certainly before layout decisions are made.

When you have chosen the photos, checked into reproduction rights, calculated costs, and organized the book in a general way, you may now proceed to the time-devouring and always daunting task of designing the book, layout after layout, spread after spread. If you have been able to find the illustrations that express your vision, the book can take on a life of its own.

In Conclusion

The tasks described in these three scenarios can be very different, yet in each, appropriate imagery properly placed will enhance the text, elucidate the narrative, or perhaps completely formulate a story line. Now that authors are commonly called upon to acquire illustrations, you need at least a working knowledge of the complexities of the task. More pictures in a book will call for more thought, more research, more money, and more creativity. As the number of images increases so, too, do the headaches involved in working through the process. The attitude among some publishers that illustrating a book is "automatic" will surely cut down on production time, but it will also likely lead to one more book looking like dozens of others. By contrast, when you go to the trouble of finding the right pictures and the right spots for them, you will not only have a superior publication, you will have fun in the process, too.

Chapter Eight

RESEARCHING
BASEBALL PHOTOGRAPHS
by Jom Shieber

Photography dates back to the late 1820s, but the first perfected process (the daguerreotype) was not made public until August of 1839. Coincidentally, that was the same year that, according to the 1907 Mills Commission, Abner Doubleday invented the game of baseball in Cooperstown, New York. While the latter date and its accompanying "history" are dubious at best, it is safe to say that baseball and photography have grown up together.

While acting quite literally as illustrative documents to enrich an article or book, baseball photographs also provide the researcher with a wealth of information. Indeed, the amount and type of information one can glean from a baseball photo is often quite surprising. As an example, in 1991 the author found that various baseball encyclopedias listed pitcher Harry Gruber, one-time 20-game winner (and two-time 20-game loser), as throwing with his left hand. However, examination of a photo of Gruber from an N-172 Old Judge cabinet card clearly shows the nineteenth-century hurler to be a right-hander.

The SABR Biographical Committee was notified of the error, and various encyclopedias made the change. Research relying heavily on subtle clues found in the background of the famous Charles Conlon photo of Ty Cobb sliding into third base helped determine the exact date of the photo—a different date than was recalled by the photographer himself!

Here are a few pointers designed to help you research baseball photographs:

Captions

A common mistake of baseball researchers is to blindly trust the caption of a photograph. Whether the caption is on an original print, part of a wire service photo, or accompanies the photo in a book: Beware the caption. Although captions often provide useful information, they are by no means infallible.

Wire service photos are generally accompanied by captions. The date on such a caption may reflect when the photo was taken, but it often corresponds to the day after the event (that is, the day the photo appeared in newspapers). Player identifications are generally reliable, but it is always wise to compare faces with verified images. The location (city and state) may indicate where the pictured event took place, but may also indicate the closest newspaper or wire service office.

Photos that were at one time part of a newspaper morgue (a reference file of old pictures, clippings, and such) are often found with articles affixed to their reverse. The attached newspaper article is usually the one that originally accompanied the photo when it ran in the paper. Clues in the article—and information from portions of other articles that may be visible—can help date a photo. However, the story may have run months or years after the photo was taken, with the newspaper simply using an old picture to illustrate the story. A stamped date found on the reverse of a file photo in the morgue usually indicates the issue date of the paper in which the photo was reproduced. Thus, it represents only an "upper limit" to the actual date of the photo.

Players' Uniforms

Be sure to examine each player's uniform closely and compare this information with the bible of the baseball photographic researcher, Marc Okkonen's *Baseball Uniforms of the 20th Century*. A word of caution regarding Marc's invaluable reference work (as well as any other source to which you refer): While errors are few and far between, they do exist. Mistakes and discrepancies occur in the best of sources.

When researching a baseball photo, don't assume that the players pictured are wearing major league uniforms—even if the player pictured is known to have been a big leaguer. The photo may pre-date his major league career, or, as was often the case in the first half of the twentieth century, it may have been taken following his days in the big leagues, as he was back in the minors, on his way down.

Many baseball photos were shot during spring training. In preseason play, it was very common for ball clubs to wear the uniforms of the previous season. Not until opening day would they unveil their brand new uniforms. Ballplayers were also more likely to "mix and match" home and road uniform components during spring training, donning the "wrong" stockings, jersey, or cap.

An example of a spring training photo with an erroneous caption is found on page 11 of Donald Honig's *The American League: An Illustrated History*. The photo shows Hall of Famer Nap Lajoie, with this caption: "Nap Lajoie soon after joining the Philadelphia Athletics in 1901." But the uniform does not match that worn by the Athletics of the early 1900s. In fact, the uniform is consistent with that worn by the A's in 1913 and 1914. Since Lajoie did not rejoin the A's until 1915, it is likely that the photo was taken in the preseason of 1915 with the Athletics wearing their old 1914 uniforms.

With black-and-white photographs it is often difficult to determine the colors of uniforms. Keep in mind that most old black-and-white photographic film recorded the color red much darker than one might expect, while blue is often lighter. Also, stripes and pinstripes may not be visible when a photograph is poorly reproduced or overexposed. For example, the famous Charles Conlon photo of Ty Cobb sliding into third base features third baseman Jimmy Austin in a New York (AL) uniform. The stockings worn by Austin may appear to be of a single, solid color, but well-reproduced versions of the photo clearly show two stripes on a dark background. The stripes were red, the background blue.

Uniform numbers are always good clues to player identifications and photo dates. To decipher uniform numbers, you can refer to the club rosters in *The Sporting News*'s annual *Dope Books* or, more conveniently and comprehensively, to Mark Stang and Linda Harkness's wonderful encyclopedia of uniform numbers, *Baseball By the Numbers*.

Ballpark Features

By noting particular features of a ballpark in the background of a photo, you can often narrow down the possible clubs and/or players pictured, as well as the era of the photo. Familiarize yourself with the classic ballparks. Comiskey Park is quickly identified by its characteristic archways beyond the field box level. The buildings beyond the outfield walls at Hilltop Park in New York and Wrigley Field in Chicago aid in their identification. The outfield walls at many parks (Fenway Park, Ebbets Field, Baker Bowl, etc.) are distinctive.

Keep in mind other facts about ballparks. Did you know that ivy did not grace the outfield walls at Wrigley until 1937? Or that from late June 1911 through the season of 1922 the upper and lower deck facades of the Polo Grounds were adorned with decorative fresco reliefs? Study pictures of these old ballparks and soon you'll be a whiz at determining photo locations.

Multiple trees in the background of a photograph are generally indicative of a photo taken during spring training. But beware—a palm tree seen beyond an outfield wall may indicate Dodger Stadium in Los Angeles, not preseason baseball in Florida.

The existence of floodlight standards (or the lack thereof) can often help to narrow down the possible dates and locations of a photo. Pay attention to other clues like the locations of supporting columns, the look of scoreboards and clocks, the existence of rooftop features—both on the ballpark and on buildings beyond the confines of the park. All of these may help you determine where and when a photo was taken.

Shadows

Look for shadows. If many shadows are present, it may be a clue that the photo was taken at a night game. If just one shadow is present, take care to note its direction. This information combined with a knowledge of which way a ballpark is oriented can help identify the location of the player or players in the photo, or, conversely, where the photographer stood to take the picture. By the 1930s, most major league ballparks were oriented so that the line from home plate toward left field pointed generally north. Thus, the late afternoon the sun would tend to cast a shadow that was parallel to the first base line, pointing out toward right field. Classic ballparks such as Fenway Park, Comiskey Park, Municipal Stadium, Tiger Stadium, Ebbets Field, Wrigley Field, Crosley Field, Shibe Park, and Sportsman's Park all followed this pattern.

However, a number of ballparks deviated from this orientation. Griffith Stadium's right field line pointed due east, for example, and the Polo Grounds' right field line pointed approximately southeast. Take a look at the famous photo of Willie Mays' great catch in the 1954 World Series. Willie was in deep center field when he made "The Catch," and his shadow points toward left field, nearly parallel to the center field wall. In most ballparks, Mays' shadow would have extended in front of him and toward the right.

Baseball Postcards

Postcards featuring baseball players can often be dated by means of the information shown on their reverse. Of course, the date found on a stamp cancellation can help provide an "upper limit" for a date. But dates can also be determined from comments in the text of the written message. Finally, don't ignore the seemingly cryptic markings, including letters and symbols, located in the upper right-hand corner of the postcard's reverse, where the postage stamp is generally placed. These markings can also date the postcard. A table explaining letter-and-symbol markings can be found in almost any book for postcard collectors, as well as at various locations on the World Wide Web.

Other Clues

When it comes to researching baseball photographs, it is wise to keep an open mind in addition to open eyes. You can often find clues to dates, locations, and player identifications in subtle and easily overlooked ways.

- ● **Grandstands and Bleachers.** Take careful note of whether the stands in the background are crowded or empty. By comparing this information with an attendance figure in the boxscore, you may be able to corroborate the date of an event. If the stands are remarkably empty, this may indicate that the photo was taken during spring training. Or it may signify a photo taken during batting practice or some other pre-game activity.

- ● **Advertising Signs.** Advertisements on outfield walls can act as photographic "fingerprints." Since ads rarely changed during the regular season, matching advertising signs with those found in a photograph with an established date can help you pinpoint the exact year in which a picture was taken.

- ● **Chalk Lines.** Pay attention to chalk lines on the ball field. For example, if a photo from the 1950s shows the catcher's position clearly marked by a triangle of chalk *by Leslie Heaphy / Chair, Women in Baseball Committee*

Women in baseball is a large category covering a wide range of topics of interest to researchers. Many committee members have focused on the individual players and teams of the All-American Girls Professional Baseball League (AAGPBL), 1943 to 1954. The AAGPBL has a Web site that provides a good introduction to the league (www.dlcwest.com/~smudge). Other popular topics for research include women umpires, bloomer teams, women executives, women in the Negro Leagues, the Colorado Silver Bullets, statistical records, and present-day women's teams.

Chapter 3, "A Checklist of Sources," lists a number of books that can serve as starting points for research of women in baseball. A book not mentioned but worth consulting is Lois Browne's *Girls of Summer: The Real Story of the All-American Girls Professional Baseball League* (HarperCollins, 1992). When the Colorado Silver Bullets were formed in 1993-94, the team evoked a great deal of media interest, with articles in major newspapers, along with many television news stories and interviews

A key place to begin is at the National Baseball Hall of Fame Library. The library has a large collection of surveys filled out by players from the AAGPBL as well as files on individual teams, record books, scrapbooks, news articles, and other materials. The library also has photographs of players and teams. If you are looking for statistical information on the AAGPBL, you will want to check out *Facts, Figures and Official Rules for Major League Baseball*, published in the 1940s by the Whitman Publishing Company. Each of these annuals contains a section at the back with the league records for the AAGPBL for that particular year.

Local newspapers provide an invaluable resource when you are looking for information about a specific team in the AAGPBL. Then, too, some communities like Grand Rapids, Michigan, and Racine, Wisconsin, have information in their local libraries and historical societies. There are some records, too, at Penn State (State College, Pennsylvania) and Rockford, Illinois. The AAGPBL has a players' association that can help in locating living players.

On some of the other topics there are not as many resources available, but old newspapers are always worth checking, as are standard baseball publications such as *The Sporting News*, which occasionally carried stories about women's baseball. The work of SABR members, especially those in the Women in Baseball Committee, continues to add to the materials available to researchers.

If you are searching for information on recent or current women's teams, the Internet becomes an indispensable resource, since the American Women's Baseball League (AWBL) and most of its teams have Web sites. Here you can find almost anything you need. AWBL's Web site (www.womenplayingbaseball.com) also contains, under "Resources," an excellent bibliography of books and articles about women in baseball.

lines, this means that the picture was taken prior to 1955. The familiar rectangular catcher's box was not introduced until that season. Also, the lack of chalk lines may indicate that the action took place later in a game, when the lines were wiped out.

❼ Distance Markings. Pay attention to distance markings on outfield walls at ballparks. These helpful numbers can aid in determining at what ballpark a photo was taken. Also, since the number can be associated with a particular outfield location (left, left-center, center, etc.), you may also be able to identify the outfielder. For example, the famous photo of Al Gionfriddo's catch in game six of the 1947 World Series clearly shows the outfield distance marking of "415 FT." Of course, the play is well documented in almost every general history of the game, but if the photo were not as well known, the outfield marking clue could be useful in determining the location of the catch.

❼ Decorative Bunting. Does a photo show decorative bunting draped over a ballpark's walls and facades? If so, you are probably looking at a World Series or All-Star game photo. Since these games are well documented, most players and locations can then be easily determined.

❼ Positions of Umpires. Imagine knowing nothing about the famous photo of Sandy Amoros's great catch in the 1955 World Series. A photo researcher will immediately be struck by two clues indicating that the photograph was taken at either an All-Star or a World Series game. First, there is decorative bunting draped over the stands in foul territory in deep left field. Second, there is an umpire just a few yards away from the play. This could only be an umpire working as part of a six-man crew—a giveaway that the game is either an All-Star or World Series contest. From 1933 to 1948, All-Star games were covered by four-man umpiring crews. The six-man crew was introduced at the mid-summer classic of 1949. As for World Series contests, four-man crews were *de rigueur* from 1903 to 1946, with the first six-man crew debuting in 1947.

❼ Modern Equipment. Is a batter or base runner wearing a batting helmet, batting gloves, or other relatively modern equipment? Clues involving equipment can help date a photo. If you need clear and concise information about the date or dates that batting helmets, batting gloves, and the like were introduced, a good source is Appendix 1 of *Total Baseball V*: "Rules and Scoring" by Dennis Bingham and Tom Heitz.

➊ **Non-baseball Clues.** Don't forget to use non-baseball clues to date a photo, if such clues are present. If automobiles appear in a picture, perhaps their style can help date a photo. The more cars in the photo the better, since one or two cars standing alone could be clunkers or antiques. Even clothing and advertising styles can help narrow down the year in which a photo was taken.

Finally, be aware that help on baseball photo research can be obtained from a number of sources. Major and local area historical societies are often good starting points. So are local libraries, newspapers, and SABR members. And don't forget SABR's own Pictorial History Committee, which is an important resource for all facets of baseball photo research.

As SABR's Publications Director, I hope that much of the output of SABR researcher-writers eventually appears in SABR publications. It is also part of my job—a part that I enjoy very much—to help members find other markets for their articles and publishers for their books. But since Larry Gerlach has done a wonderful job discussing the general publication process in Chapter 10, "Preparing the Manuscript for Publication," I am going to limit myself here to the perspective of SABR publications and the typical SABR researcher-writer. Much of this material appears on the SABR Web site, www.sabr.org, where it will be updated as needed.

SABR PUBLICATIONS

SABR's membership publications are written mainly by members and for members. From sixty to eighty articles are published in *The Baseball Research Journal* (*BRJ*) or *The National Pastime* (*TNP*) each year. Occasionally one of these SABR journals will publish the work of someone who is a nonmember or a lapsed member. If I want an article that only a nonmember can do or has done, I will take it. SABR has recently begun a program of annual books, of which *Addie Joss: King of the Pitchers*, *Uncle Robbie*, and *Lefty Grove: American Original* are the first three. Only SABR members are considered as authors for these books.

Editorial Choices

SABR publications are not scholarly works as that term is understood in the academic world, although many articles in both *TNP* and *BRJ* are the result of serious scholarly effort over a long period of time. The SABR publications program is inclusive. It gives members a reasonable shot at being published. The annual journals are, in effect, magazines—repositories of articles on a range of topics. Nobody is going to like everything in the journals, but I try to make sure that there is good editorial balance so that everybody will find plenty to enjoy.

With a few exceptions, SABR membership publications have limited commercial appeal. Our recent distribution arrangement with the University of Nebraska Press will get our publications—the books, especially—on the shelves of more libraries and bookstores around the country, but it remains our purpose to publish good work that larger publishers can't find a market for. It is safe to say that SABR will not be publishing books for a broad general market.

All SABR articles are read and checked by at least three, and usually four, people besides the author. Aside from the Publications Director, all readers are SABR volunteers, and most are well known throughout SABR for their depth and breadth of knowledge. They work hard for the Society, and they do a terrific job. Our goal is perfection, and we work hard to achieve it, but the reality is that we cannot realistically expect to compete with, say, *The New Yorker*'s paid staff of expert fact checkers.

Errors do occur, and they bother me a lot. I wish we had a good way to address mistakes when they appear in print, but annuals really don't lend themselves to letters to the editor or correction columns. I continue to look for a good way to handle comments, addenda, errata, and the other good interactive stuff that can help make readers feel a publication really belongs to them. Eventually, the Internet may be the solution, but the majority of SABR members aren't yet online (I think it's about 50-50), and I'm reluctant to engage in cyberspace conversations that most members aren't privy to. Of course, if an article is later reprinted in a book or online, any errors in it can be corrected at that time. Unfortunately, only a very few articles are ever reprinted—and they tend to be ones without significant errors.

I line edit each of the thirty to forty articles that make up our annuals, reorganizing where I think it's necessary. Except in extraordinary circumstances, I do not do serious rewrites. I send problem articles back with specific comments and suggestions. Sometimes the author takes care of the problem. Sometimes I never hear from him or her again. I may bounce a piece back a second or even a third time, if that seems necessary. My aim is to treat SABR authors with respect, and also to ensure that the articles that appear in print are theirs, not mine.

Certain authors appear regularly. The reason is simple: They continue to send in material that I think the membership will be interested in. Certain authors don't appear as often as I would like—or at all. The reasons vary. Some object to the fact that payment consists of only two free copies of the publication plus the right to buy more copies at half price. Some consider their research ongoing, and seem never to be ready to publish. Others are working on lengthy projects and don't want to take the time to polish a short piece. With each of these holdouts I remain hopeful that someday....

There is no arbitrary word or page limit. My general advice is to "write as much as the topic needs." But I often do give specific advice on particular topics. Certain things aren't, to my mind, worth five pages. Others, to my mind, are worth ten.

Editors of publications such as *The Negro Leagues Book* or *Baseball's First Stars* are typically offered a small stipend. This has been somewhat controversial as a matter of principle—there are those who feel that SABR members doing SABR projects should not receive payment. Some editors have refused the stipend. But strictly as a financial matter, these payments, when they are made, amount to pennies per hour for the work required.

I continue to use brief author blurbs in the journals, not so that authors can impress us all with their qualifications (most of the short bios are either workaday or humorous), but because I think SABR members like to get to know each other, and this is one way to help that happen. Authors can say pretty much what they want to say about themselves. The best way to judge what to say is simply to look at what other authors have said in the past. The articles and authors that are featured ("teased" in magazine parlance) on the front cover typify good work on a wide and balanced range of topics—a strong, representative sample of what's inside. They are not necessarily "the best" articles in the publication, although they are always among the best. Over the past few years, I've been trying to link the cover with a strong lead article. No author has yet asked me to feature his article on the cover. I hope it stays that way.

Photos and Design

Illustrations come mainly from three sources: the author, the National Baseball Library, or Mark Rucker at Transcendental Graphics. I've been using mostly Transcendental Graphics recently because the process of working with Mark is more direct and the price is comparable. Both he and the NBL are friendly, helpful, and offer a special deal to SABR. There has not been, contrary to myth, some massive SABR Photo Archive dug deep into the ground under Woodbury, Connecticut, or Cleveland, Ohio. However, SABR has acquired the Minneapolis Photo Collection, and SABR publications may eventually make great use of these images.

Although I work with a freelance cover designer who uses the image and teasers of my choice, SABR has no art director. Therefore, the interior design of the annuals is fairly standardized. That won't change. I'm kicking around some basic redesign ideas, but it would be a complex and perhaps overly ambitious task to create multiple options within a general design concept. I use a simple, serviceable template, within which I can create a basic layout for *BRJ* and *TNP*.

The editorial schedule for the annuals is a 100-day countdown that incorporates editorial, design, layout, production elements, sending and receiving page proofs and contracts, following up on authors who don't respond in a timely fashion, double-checking disputed facts, dealing with the printer, and handling the inevitable emergencies and foulups. All this happens while the next book begins to form on a parallel track, and a fairly heavy stream of correspondence arrives from potential authors and members needing information. SABR publications come out on time—but often just barely.

BASIC INFORMATION FOR SABR AUTHORS: *Queries*

For your own sake, don't go to all the trouble of writing an article before you touch base with the Publications Director, who is also the editor of most SABR publications. Query first. Call or write with a proposal, an outline, or both, setting out your idea for an article. I (or occasionally an appointed publication editor) will give you an honest appraisal of your idea, perhaps some suggestions, and will tell you if we'd like to see a manuscript.

This doesn't necessarily mean that your article will be published. I may find that it doesn't stick to the point that your query promised, or even (heaven forbid!) that it's too poorly written for salvation. But querying does prevent you for doing a lot of work on something that I simply don't think will work for the publication in the first place.

Please do not send: (a) a list of multiple article possibilities, (b) a rough draft, or (c) a long piece with the suggestion that I "edit it down." You should also rethink and rework term papers and theses before submitting them. The SABR audience knows more about baseball and responds to more idiomatic writing than do most professors.

Email

Feel free to send queries—not full articles—by email to me at sabrpubs@aol.com, although I'm also happy to receive them by U.S. Mail at P.O. Box 736, Woodbury, CT 06798. For security reasons I don't open an email attachment unless I am specifically expecting it.

Format for Hard Copy

- Use a single standard font throughout and keep your format simple.
- Double-space your manuscript.
- Include a word count.
- Leave generous margins all around a roughly twenty-five-line page. This makes your manuscript easy to read, and it leaves room for notes in the margins.
- Start typing your manuscript about halfway down the first page. This leaves space for even more notes at the top of your copy.
- Make sure the top of every page carries your last name and the page number.
- If you're using a computer, don't set your word-processing program to justify text (this means making every line the same length, as in a book). Your manuscript should be ragged right (i.e., left alignment), as in standard typewritten documents. The reason? It's much easier for the editor working with hard copy to verify your word count from a non-justified manuscript.
- If you plan to submit your manuscript on a computer disk, please refer to the instructions below under "Computer Disks, Email Attachments." You'll save a lot of time—for yourself and for SABR—by formatting your manuscript from the beginning so that the editor can work easily and effectively from the disk.

Photos, Graphics, Tables, and Charts

If you have photos, send photocopies of them along with the hard copy, so I'll know what I've got to work with. Sometimes researchers come up with wonderful cartoons or drawings. I'd like to see those, too. If your article requires tables or charts, build them carefully, and be sure they make their point clearly (a surprising number don't). Please build your charts using tabs or the "Table" function offered by most word processors, not a sequence of taps on the spacebar. Graphs should be "camera ready"—that is, they should be clear enough to be shot and printed as submitted. If any reduction is size is needed, it cannot be so great that the print becomes too small to read.

Style

The standard stylebooks (the *Chicago Manual of Style* and the *MLA Style Manual* are two of many examples) differ on many questions. Over the years SABR has put together its own style manual, partly to cover the many baseball terms not covered by the others. Our toughest challenge is numbers, because they show up so often in so many forms and types. Our Golden Rule for numbers is to try to use words where every kind of writing except sportswriting would use words, but use figures when dealing with the unique statistical elements of baseball. Some specifications:

- Spell out all numbers under 100.
- Spell out players' ages and heights.
- Spell out numbers in quoted speech.
- Spell out numbers beginning a sentence.
- Spell out decades.
- Spell out number of games ahead or behind in team standings.
- Spell out numerical expressions, such as "Two or three hundred years ago."
- Use figures for numbers above 99, for dates, dimensions, and tallies (such as votes for Hall of Fame.)
- Use a comma or commas in four-figure or larger numbers.
- Avoid ordinals (8th, 15th) for dates, but usages such as "53rd double" or "714th home run" are permissible.

You can find the SABR Style Sheet at www.sabr.org

In recent years, questions have begun to arise about electronic style—how to spell email (not Email or e-mail); how to indicate Web sites (forget the http:// and start with www.); how to write email addresses (all lower case), and so forth. In general, we try to follow the advice in *Wired Style: Principles of English Usage in the Digital Age*, available at most bookstores and on the Internet.

Notes and Sources

Most SABR articles require a list of sources (usually a short bibliography, sometimes including acknowledgements of interview subjects or other particularly helpful individuals). Many require citations, which is SABR journals means endnotes. Our general rule is that the notes should be references, not expansions on the text. In our relatively short articles, if information is worth conveying, it's worth including in the text. (We sometimes break this rule in longer pieces.) Check the *MLA Style Manual* for appropriate form for notes and bibliographies.

The *MLA Style Manual* is available in every library, it can be purchased inexpensively on-line or in bookstores, and it is available on the Web at www.mla.org/set_stl.htm/. A good Web site on the why and how of citations, called "Sources, Their Use and Acknowledgment," is available at www.dartmouth.edu/~sources/.

Copyright

If your article is accepted, you will receive a letter of agreement with your page proofs (see below), which will make several points clear. The two main ones are that (1) you retain copyright, and (2) you grant SABR first serial rights and the right to use the article in any future SABR anthologies. ("First serial rights" means the legal right of SABR to be the first to publish your article in a periodical. You could not grant first serial rights, for instance, if your piece had already appeared in, for example, *Baseball Digest*.)

Response Time

How long should you wait for a response? I try to get back to you within a few days of receiving any sort of communication. But the office is small, the work load is large, and I sometimes fall behind in my correspondence. If you don't hear from me in a month, give me a call, send an email, or write an indignant note.

Author's Page Proofs

You will receive an edited, typeset copy of your article before it goes to press. Note any problems on it and return it to me. If the problems are serious, get back to me by phone as so we can work them out together.

WHICH SABR PUBLICATION?

SABR publishes four membership publications a year, two journals and two paperback books.

The *Baseball Research Journal* is SABR's original publication. Virtually all statistical studies go in the *Journal*, and, although we don't want to turn it into an academic organ, you should include notes, bibliographies, etc., where appropriate. Short articles focused on long-departed historical figures or events are okay here, but they must have a strong analytical approach. This is also the place for articles focusing technically, as opposed to historically, on the business of baseball or on playing techniques.

The National Pastime is just what John Thorn's original subtitle calls it—"a review of baseball history." The articles in it don't require a strong analytical edge and are usually more anecdotal than those in *BRJ*. This doesn't mean that we don't expect solid research on historical subjects for *TNP*, just that there's more room here for speculation, opinion, nostalgia, humor, poetry, and a certain amount of writing culled from non-SABR sources. There's some overlap between the two publications. Some articles can go either way, and if that's the case with yours, your editor will suggest which one seems more appropriate.

The two books SABR puts out each year vary widely in approach and subject matter. Some of them are committee publications: *The Negro Leagues Book*, for example. Others are reprints, such as *Baseball: How to Become a Player*, by John Montgomery Ward. Still others are works of original research, like Scott Longert's biography of pitcher Addie Joss; or collections of photos and text, like *Baseball for the Fun of It*, by Mark Rucker, Tom Shieber, and Mark Alvarez. We are always looking for good ideas.

Timely Publication

When an article is accepted for publication, I usually tell you where and when we want to run it. Sometimes I get so much good material that I'm forced to say when I accept it that it may have to be held over for one of next year's publications.

Occasionally, I discover as I get into the editorial process and start assembling an issue of *BRJ* or *TNP* that I have to take one or more articles out and move them to the next year's edition. This is sometimes a matter of space and sometimes a matter of balance (too much about the National League in the 1950s, too little about nineteenth century baseball). Deferring an article in this way is not a signal that I don't like it. (If I accepted it, I want to run it!) Any delay of this kind is never a casual decision, because I know how hard you've worked and how eager you are to see your article in print. And I never do it without notifying you, apologizing for the disappointment it may cause, and offering to free you from your letter of agreement (although I hope you'll agree to let the article run a year later than you had expected).

Computer Disks, & Email Attachments

If your article is accepted, I will ask you to send a disk or an email attachment in order to save SABR the time and expense of having the article rekeyboarded. This is a convenience for me, not an absolute necessity. If you don't have a computer, that's okay.

I handle all editing and layout in the SABR Publications Office. I translate all manuscripts into Microsoft Word 98 for the Mac, rough edit them, and then flow them into Adobe PageMaker 6.5 for final editing and layout. For reasons both financial and technical, graphs and photos are stripped in mechanically by the printer.

RESEARCH ON BALLPARKS

by Bob Bluthardt / Chair, Ballparks Committee

Ballparks have become a very popular topic in baseball research, and the SABR Ballparks Committee stands ready to assist anyone seeking information, guidance, and contacts. The committee was established in 1982 at the annual SABR Convention and has grown to nearly 275 members. The committee newsletter, published three or four times annually, outlines available articles, ongoing projects, and new members with their interests. It also summarizes ballpark-related news at the major and minor league levels.

The committee library has a number of standard ballparks reference books, as well as dozens of monographs, programs, and lesser-known publications. We also maintain a regularly updated list of books that have been published about major stadiums. Committee projects have resulted in "Ballparks in Movies & TV," an article that outlines the many parks profiled for a moment or longer on the big and small screen; and "Nineteenth Century Ballparks," which contains several short essays on the cities and their pre-1909 parks.

City Baseball Magic, a committee project by member Phil Bess, was first printed ten years ago and is available from both the committee and the publisher, Knothole Press. *CBM*, which summarizes the case for the classic "urban style" ballpark, is a valuable reference for architects, planners, and fans of the traditional ballpark.

In addition to vertical files on cities and other ballpark-related topics, the committee maintains several modest photo and slide collections documenting current and now-lost parks. A new project seeks to assemble the basic data on every minor league ballpark in history. Many members pursue their own projects and are willing to share information and resources.

Researching any ballpark or stadium is, at best, an inexact science. Typically, you can find interesting information from an in-depth look at the team or teams that played there and biographies of the star players who called the ballpark home. Also, it pays to consider the park as just another building and, therefore, to explore such resources as deeds, architects' records, building permits, inspection records, and other municipal documents.

Artists, photographers, and model makers have adopted the ballpark as a prime topic, and the committee maintains ties with some of the more prolific image makers. Many of the resources listed in chapters of this book, such as those by Andy McCue, Ted Hathaway, and Mark Rucker, will turn up ballpark photos; but the mother lode of classic photos can be found in the Bain Collection at the Library of Congress in the Prints Division.

I can translate most DOS/Windows and Mac word processing applications, but not dedicated word processor disks like those from Brother or Panasonic. I prefer not to deal with spreadsheet, database, or graphics applications.

Don't hesitate to ask me any questions you have about the use of your computer in working on a SABR manuscript. Just give me a call. But for now, here are a few tips that can make life easier at the editing stage:

- Put your name, as well as the title of your article, on the disk you send.
- Be sure to include your name and address on the first page of the document. Set up your program so that you include your last name with the page number on every page of the hard copy. That way, if I drop a pile of manuscripts—it has happened—I can put things back together quite easily.
- Use your last name to name your file. It's much easier for me to keep track of things if the author's name appears, not the name of the topic or some other abbreviation. Thus, use SMITH.TXT or JONES.DOC, for example, rather than RBIRUTH.LOT, or some such.
- Use a plain, simple format. Please don't choose fancy fonts, and don't overuse italic or bold text. Don't center or flush-right anything—even titles or subheads. Simple, old-fashioned, flush-left, plain text is always best.
- Use a single space between sentences, not the two spaces required in typewriting. On a computer, the program automatically spaces properly after a period.
- Don't use a tab or a series of spacebar hits at the beginning of each paragraph. Use a setup that automatically indents—or don't indent at all. My applications will automatically indent.
- Let your computer handle the "carriage return" at the end of each line. If you strike the RETURN key, you are specifying a new paragraph.
- Don't leave a line space between paragraphs by striking the ENTER or the RETURN key twice.
- Graphs and charts must arrive in camera-ready form (as they will be seen in the publication). I can resize them mechanically, but I can't output them from computer files.
- Use your spell checker. Pay close attention to every word that is shown as being erroneously spelled. Check the word against a standard dictionary if you still have doubts.
- **VERY IMPORTANT.** When you create a table, please, please, please use a tab, not a series of spacebar hits to line things up. Don't worry if that makes the columns look one space (or more) out of line. If you use just a single tab between columns, all will be well when the material reaches PageMaker. If you

use the spacebar, you can cause what is sometimes astonishing trouble. I sometimes have to send tables back for reformatting.

TIPS ON STYLE AND TECHNIQUE

In Chapter 10, "Preparing the Manuscript for Publication," Larry Gerlach covers some of what follows. My comments here are specific to writers contributing to SABR's annual journals. The suggestions grow out of my experience in editing these publications, and I hope that any overlap will serve as emphasis.

1. **Be yourself**. More than anything else, this is the key to good writing. Let your personality come through. We're a band of friends in SABR. We want to hear from you. Being real in writing doesn't undercut your expertise one bit. Simply put, write the way you talk. Read your text out loud to yourself. If it doesn't sound the way you normally sound, fix it. Here are some specifics:

   - Don't get formal, pompous, or prissy just because your thoughts are going down on paper.
   - Where you have a choice, use the short word rather than the long one.
   - Chop most adjectives and adverbs. Instead, try to find nouns and verbs that are precise enough not to need modifiers.
   - Keep your paragraphs fairly short.
   - Use the active voice. Don't write, "It can be observed . . ." Write, "You can see . . ." or "Working with these numbers I noticed. . . ." In short, sound confident, not mealy-mouthed.

2. **Have a point**. I mean this literally. You're writing an article, not a book. You have to stay focused on your main idea. Sounds obvious, I know, but it's surprising how fuzzy a lot of us are on defining exactly what we're up to. Try explaining your main idea in a brief sentence. If you can't, you've got a problem.

3. **Answer a question, don't confirm a prejudice**. We often get queries and articles from writers with an axe to grind, who use only the facts, stats, or anecdotes that support their side of an argument. We reject these quickly. We want a point of view, and we like it to be colorfully expressed, but it must be based on all the facts available, not on a determined marshaling of only one side of the case.

4. **Prune extraneous material**. This speaks to one of the great flaws in a remarkably high percentage of SABR writing. I know how tempting it is to stuff in all the neat things you've dug up in your research. But it's important to remember

that not all this nifty data is relevant to the one point you're trying to hammer home. The material you've collected won't disappear, after all. You may be able to use it later in an article where it really fits.

5. **Don't strain for a lead paragraph.** This probably contradicts other advice you've received over the years. But I've found time after time that good SABR leads emerge later in an article, and that heavily worked-over and strained-for opening paragraphs simply get lopped off because they're too artificial. Try jumping right into your topic. Just say what it is you've found, or what you want to demonstrate, or what historical event you want to describe. This opening may not in the end remain the first paragraph of your article, but it lets you get into your writing smoothly and easily, saving you a lot of mental anguish. Chances are, a natural lead will emerge as you write. You may not recognize it, but your editor usually will.

6. **Imagine you're writing a letter to a friend.** This can help if you're having trouble getting going, or if you're a little intimidated by the idea of being published. In fact, this approach often results in the very best kind of articles—personal, colorful, and idiomatic.

7. **Rewrite.** Your first draft is just that. Go though your article carefully to make sure it is well organized. I often get manuscripts in which the writers have tacked things on as they've thought of them, rather than taking the time to rewrite and put them where they belong. Your rewrite is the place to make sure you sound like you. It is also the time to confirm that your sentences really say what you want them to say.

8. **Stop when you've said what needs to be said.** A great concluding sentence sets off an article like the cherry on top of a hot fudge sundae. But remember that the sundae tastes pretty good even without the cherry. If you've got a quick, catchy conclusion, by all means use it. But if you're straining to be funny, or simply summarizing or restating what you've already written, forget it. (As with your article's lead, your true conclusion is likely to be lurking somewhere else in your manuscript. If you can't find it, maybe your editor can.)

9. **Call your editor.** If you're having trouble, call. If you want to change your approach, call. If you just want to chat, call. The publications staff, whether permanent or free-lance, is here to help you. We all want the same thing—outstanding SABR articles in outstanding SABR publications—and a good publishing experience for everyone.

10. **_Expect to be edited_**. Very few nonfiction pieces are ever printed by any publication exactly as written. Although SABR doesn't require articles to meet an arbitrary word count, it sometimes happens that a piece has to be cut to fit the available space. Good editors (like us, we hope) do this very gingerly. Your editor may do a number of other things, too.

THE EDITOR'S TASK

Many manuscripts contain unnecessary material (see #4 above). If so, the editor cuts text to improve the article. Sometimes, organization needs a little work. Editors move text around. Clarity can often be improved. Editors do a little judicious rewriting. Now and then, editors must find new leads or concluding paragraphs. Occasionally, when the editor feels that too many threads are left hanging loose, he will return the article, with specific comments, for more work.

This whole process can be painful and even infuriating for any writer (believe me—I know from personal experience!). But keep a few things in mind. First, your SABR editor isn't just trying to get his fingerprints on your work. He is trying to improve its presentation. Second, there's nothing personal in an edit. Changes to your carefully wrought prose aren't intended as an affront to your talent, your integrity, or your manhood. Third, writers, because they're intimately wrestling with their topic, often lack a sense of perspective about their work. It's the editor's job to look at the forest as well as the trees. Give your editor the benefit of the doubt.

Nonetheless, editors sometimes make mistakes. That's why SABR will send you a set of page proofs—a copy of your printed article—before publication. This gives you a chance to get in touch with your editor about any problems you see and to iron them out. No writer should ever be surprised by what he finds in print under his byline.

Not all researchers want to publish an article or a book. For them, the joy of research is satisfaction enough. Others choose less formal means than periodicals or books to disseminate research—for example, making oral presentations at regional or national SABR meetings, depositing copies of their work with the SABR Research Papers Collection, mailing photocopies of the material to others interested in the subject, or posting findings on the Internet. All of these are effective means of sharing research.

SABR-L, online, is an especially useful forum for time-sensitive research, especially statistical analyses of player or team performances such as the McGwire-Sosa home run race in 1998. For information on SABR-L (and on a host of other SABR services, regional groups, committees, and awards) see the front pages of the most recent *SABR Membership Directory.*

Surveying the Market

Let's say you do want to see your work in print. You should ask yourself two basic questions before beginning to write:

❷ Is my research publishable?
❷ If so, what is the best publisher for it?

Unfortunately, not everyone who would like to publish his or her research is able to do so. Some topics have been covered adequately by previous studies—there may be no interest in another biography of Billy Martin—and sometimes a book or article on the same subject appears, or has already been accepted. As a SABR member, you will find it pays to belong to one or more research committees. That way you can learn who (at least in the Society) is already researching a specific topic in your area of expertise.

Some projects are too limited in scope to appeal to a publisher. A study of your grandfather's two seasons as a backup catcher with the Salt Lake City Bees of the PCL will generate little interest outside your family. Similarly, a statistical formula that adjusts the slugging percentages of Western League batters in 1949 according to differences in the altitudes of the ballparks will almost certainly fall on deaf ears in publishing circles.

One way to get a good sense of the publication potential of your work, as well as to get an idea of possible publishers, is to compare your proposed project with existing articles and books in the same subject area. You can then contact the editors of journals (including SABR's) or book publishing companies to determine their possible interest in what you have to offer. Editors generally prefer queries of this kind to arrive by letter or email rather than by phone. They don't want to make snap judgments, something that a phone call inevitably invites. A written query will normally receive a written response. Ideally, this response will indicate the editor's interest, but even if it's negative it may offer suggestions for publication alternatives.

When making an inquiry, be sure to explain in detail the nature and significance of your work. Many topics are inherently interesting, but editors want to know what is special about your proposed project. Is this the first study of your particular topic? Does it offer new information on a familiar topic, or a new interpretation of it? Take care in crafting your letter. How well you present your idea and yourself can influence an editor's assessment of the project. Although editorial expressions of interest are not commitments to publish, they do indicate that the editor likes what you're doing and wants to consider the completed manuscript. You will never get a firm acceptance from a preliminary inquiry, but you may receive a rejection. In that case, promptly send off your query to another publisher.

Journal editors usually determine their interest in seeing the manuscript on the basis of a simple inquiry. Book publishers, on the other hand, may ask for an introduction, an outline, and a couple of sample chapters. They will also want to know how your work compares with existing books on the same or a closely related subject, particularly those than have been published recently. How, for example, does your biography of Honus Wagner differ from the several excellent ones now in print?

Most baseball projects don't require a literary agent. If you have a book-length manuscript with high sales potential, one that may be of interest to large commercial publishers, you might want to consider getting a literary agent. But remember, major book publishers are looking primarily for blockbusters, and very few baseball books, even the best ones, fit into that category.

Article or Book?

Obviously, you have to decide whether your research project is one that will result in an article or a book. Your target audience, the nature of your research (statistical, historical, or biographical), and the length of the planned manuscript will help you determine an appropriate publisher. If you're writing a short piece of statistical analysis, like Stuart

Shapiro's "Predicting Postseason Results," for a baseball-savvy audience, your choice will almost certainly be *The Baseball Research Journal*. If you're writing a complete history of night baseball, like David Pietrusza's *Lights On!: The Wild Century-Long Saga of Night Baseball*, for a general audience of baseball fans, your choice may be a commercial book publisher such as Scarecrow Press. If you're writing what is prospectively the definitive biography of Lou Gehrig, like Ray Robinson's *Iron Horse: Lou Gehrig and His Time*, you may attract a major commercial house such as W.W. Norton (HarperCollins, paperback).

Articles

The great majority of SABR research manuscripts are of article length, which is to say ten to thirty pages of double-spaced, typewritten material. Many of these manuscripts are written specifically for *The Baseball Research Journal* or *The National Pastime*, which Mark Alvarez, SABR's Publications Director, discusses at some length in Chapter 9.

There are other possibilities, too. For longer pieces, in particular, consider baseball-oriented journals like *Elysian Fields Quarterly* and *Nine: A Journal of Baseball History and Social Policy Perspectives*. Less formal publications such as SABR research committee newsletters and privately published anthologies like Herman Krabbenhoft's *Baseball Quarterly Review* and Joseph Wayman's *Grandstand Baseball Annual* contain excellent research. *Baseball Digest*, a journalistic-style monthly, publishes short, punchy articles, mostly with a biographical or statistical focus.

Fan magazines, scorecards, and yearbooks issued by major and minor league clubs are logical outlets for team-specific research. State and historical society journals, which contain a mix of scholarly and popular writing, may publish your work. And don't forget general interest periodicals, including airline magazines and newspaper supplements.

Books

It is more difficult to get a book published than it is an article for the self-evident reason that a great many more articles than books are published each year. At the same time, book publishing offers several options for you to consider.

Commercial Publishers. As their name indicates, commercial publishers are in the business of making money. The publisher assumes the basic cost of production, promotion, and distribution, paying you a modest royalty, usually about ten percent of the retail price of the book. Relatively few books break even, let alone make money, but the potential profitability of a book is a key consideration in commercial publishing. Generally speaking, a few books on most major publishers' lists earn a substantial amount of money for both author and publisher. Baseball books, however, are seldom among them.

The larger the commercial house, the greater the sales and profit expectations. If your book is likely to attract a wide audience, as, say, a biography of Jackie Robinson or a history of the New York Yankees, a large publisher may be a possibility. Otherwise, think of smaller commercial publishers, a number of which specialize in baseball books. Among them are Diamond Communications, McFarland & Company, and Scarecrow Press.

University Presses. University presses are more likely to accept manuscripts on the basis of quality and importance than on profit projections. And their editorial boards, composed primarily of faculty members, are more likely to make their decisions based on academic and scholarly attributes. When David W. Zang was unable to find a commercial publisher, he sent his manuscript to the University of Nebraska Press, which accepted and published it. Zang won SABR's first Seymour Book Award for *Fleet Walker's Divided Heart: The Life of Baseball's First Black Major Leaguer*.

Recently, university presses have begun issuing more nonacademic, general-interest books to increase revenue. The University of Nebraska Press offers a growing line of original baseball books, including Hobe Hays's *Take Two and Hit to Right: Golden Days on the Semi-Pro Diamond*. Southern Illinois University Press, too, has recently published some baseball books, including Jerry Klinkowitz'a *Owning a Piece of the Minors*. So has Temple University Press, with Robin Roberts and C. Paul Rogers III's *The Whiz Kids and the 1950 Pennant* and several others.

Many university presses take a special interest in regional history. Thus, Texas Christian University Press published Jeff Guinn and Bobby Bragan's *When Panthers Roared: The Fort Worth Cats and Minor League Baseball*. Rutgers University Press published James M. DiClerico and Barry J. Pavelic's *The Jersey Game: The History of Modern Baseball from Its Birth to the Big Leagues in the Garden State*. It's probably safe to assume that a university press in California would be more interested in a book about the Pacific Coast League than would a publisher, whether academic or commercial, in Texas or New Jersey.

Self-publishing. Always popular with baseball researchers, self-publishing has increased in recent years. Authors publish their own books because (a) it is the only realistic way to have them published and/or (b) they want to control editorial and production decisions. Commercial publishers shy away from local or regional studies and biographies of non-star players, no matter how excellent the writing or how valuable the contribution to baseball history. Even university presses prefer baseball books with broader appeal than many of the excellent self-published books now in print.

The quality of self-published books varies greatly, but the majority of these publications are valuable contributions to baseball literature. Some excellent examples are Richard E. Beverage's *The Hollywood Stars: Baseball in Movieland, 1926-1957*; Frank M. Keetz's *The Mohawk Colored Giants of Schenectady*; Vi Owen's *The Adventures of a Quiet Soul: A Scrapbook of Memories* [about her brother, Marv Owen, Detroit Tiger third baseman in the '30s] and Henry W. Thomas's *Walter Johnson: Baseball's Big Train*.

There are pluses and minuses to self-publishing. The primary advantage is that your book will appear exactly as you wrote and packaged it. It is literally your book. You decide page size and paper stock, layout and type font, number and placement of illustrations, *by James J. Combs / Chair, Baseball in UK/Europe Committee*

In the United Kingdom/Europe, the focus of research is twofold—the origins of ball-and-stick games and the history of baseball in European countries since its early development in the United States. The sources for the origin of ball-and-stick games are wide-ranging, including art history and sociological treatises, whereas the sources for the development of European baseball since 1840 are less academic.

One example of the diversity of sources for the origin of baseball is a Renaissance tapestry (found by Mike Ross, president of the Bobby Thomson Chapter) showing a shepherd and shepherdesses playing a ball-and-stick game not unlike croquet. This tapestry is important in that it tends to confirm the hypothesis that ball games and courtship were linked in the Middle Ages and Renaissance. Accordingly, the museums and libraries of Europe can be fertile sources for evidence of the origins of ball-and-stick games.

Other sources are villages where old ball games (or a version of them) are still played today. An example of one of these games is stool ball, which, as Martin Hoerchner wrote in *BRJ*99, could well be the predecessor of both cricket and "rounders" or "feeder." Stool ball is played in the villages of Hampshire in south central England, and members of the Bobby Thomson Chapter have watched games there. Another such game is trap ball, which has attracted the interest not only of our UK/Europe SABR members but also of a cricket scholar and at least one Japanese baseball scholar. Since the origins of cricket, like those of baseball, are rather mysterious, research efforts of our chapter members and cricket scholars have sometimes been collaborative.

Sources of information on the development of games similar to American baseball in the United Kingdom include scrapbooks kept by members of teams and passed down to their descendents. Newspaper accounts of the activities of indigenous leagues and teams are useful sources as well. Recently, our members have corresponded with a corporate archivist whose company is reported to have sponsored a trophy that was awarded to the winning team in one of the local leagues.

Efforts have also been made to obtain information from soccer clubs, since these clubs once sought to use baseball as an off-season training exercise for their players. While local newspapers are a fertile source of information on the activities of teams and leagues, newspapers with a national circulation have recorded several celebrated baseball games played in the United Kingdom by major league teams from the U.S. Finally, there are individuals who have played in the earlier European leagues still to be interviewed. Not long ago we interviewed the soccer player who tried to act on the advice of Babe Ruth to organize British soccer players so as to obtain better pay!

cover design, and so on. The main disadvantages are that you incur considerable out-of-pocket expenses; you usually lack editorial, design, and clerical assistance; and you are responsible for advertising, publicity, accounting, and storage.

Think of self-publishing as a business venture. You will make money if the book sells well, lose money if it doesn't. In either case, though, your overhead is far lower than that of a commercial or university press publisher, and your break-even point is correspondingly low. Moreover, the expenses incurred in researching, writing, designing, and printing the book are tax deductible.

The production quality of self-published books varies considerably. Some authors use commercial printers, thereby receiving some assistance with design (often minimal) to produce paperback books with perfect binding (glued, with a spine) similar to the trade paperbacks sold in bookstores. Self-published hardcover books such as Thomas's *Walter Johnson* are rare because of high costs. Relatively short volumes, printed or photocopied, may be fastened with staples, as are Rodney Johnson's *Arizona Baseball Journal* and Lyle Spatz's *Baseball Records Update 1993*. Photocopied pages may be bound with binding strips, as is Joseph Wayman's *Grandstand Baseball Annual*, or comb-fasteners, as are Carlos Bauer and Bob Hoie's *The Historical Register* and SABR's *The Minor League Baseball Research Journal*. Comb-binding, which can be done commercially but is usually done privately with a moderately priced machine, is (along with strip binding) the least expensive way to publish, because you simply produce as many copies as you want.

Self-publishing can be rewarding, both personally and financially, and it enables you to learn first-hand about every aspect of book publishing. But don't jump in blindly. Before deciding to self-publish, contact several authors who have done so to discuss their experiences. Also, read a good book on the subject. One of the best is Dan Poynter's (self-published) *The Self-Publishing Manual*, now in its umpteenth edition.

Vanity Presses. These represent a variation on self-publishing. These presses accept all business, do no editing, and have no credibility in the book business. You, as author, still fund the project—printing costs, advertising expenses, and distribution arrangements all remain your obligations—but you also pay a price to have the vanity press handle the production of your book for you. Vanity presses have a poor reputation and are not a good option for baseball researchers.

SABR Publications. This subject has been extensively covered by Mark Alvarez in Chapter 9, "Writing for SABR," and will not be reprised here. But, needless to say, SABR has been one of the premier publishers of baseball articles and books since its founding by Bob Davids in 1971.

GETTING READY TO WRITE

Once you have decided to try to publish your work and have thought about a potential publisher, you must put pen to paper and produce a publishable manuscript.

Researching is fun; writing is work. Gathering information is easy; turning research notes into a publishable manuscript is difficult. Research is eventually completed; writing ceases but is never finished.

Researchers sometimes find writing onerous because they already know the results of their inquiry. It can be difficult to generate enthusiasm for writing once you've learned the answer—the origins of Tony Lazzeri's famous nickname, say, or the impact of lowering the pitching mound in 1969. Others find the task intimidating because they have had little or no experience in writing for publication.

Remember that the most prolific and accomplished writers were once novices. Remember, too, that writing, while a creative art, isn't brain surgery. You can do it if you put your mind to it. Preparing a publishable manuscript will be much easier if you follow a couple of basic rules.

RULE ONE: BE PREPARED

No one—not Roger Angell, nor Roger Kahn, nor you—just sits down and begins to write. Some common-sense initial preparations will ease the process and produce better results.

First, if you are writing with a particular journal or book publisher in mind, ask the editor for a style sheet or an author's guide. You will save a lot of time and make a good impression if you prepare the manuscript according to the preferred format. Should you include footnotes or not? If so, what footnote form should you use (e.g., only the place and name of the publication or also the publisher?). Should America's famous newspaper of record appear as *The New York Times*, the *New York Times*, or the New York *Times*? Most publications, including SABR's, have specific requirements for statistical charts and tables. Follow them carefully. You can usually determine style preferences by looking at articles recently published in the journal or by the book publisher, but it's best to ask for a style sheet anyway.

Second, have a good college dictionary handy, or even an unabridged dictionary, and a serviceable thesaurus. Also be sure you have a good thesaurus—the ones that list entries alphabetically are easy to use. For book-length manuscripts, and indeed for general use, you will find a comprehensive style manual to be a useful supplement to the style sheet of the publisher. *The Chicago Manual of Style* has been a standard guide for writers and publishers since 1906. Be sure to use the latest edition. A less comprehensive but widely used manual that covers the basics is Kate Turabian's *A Manual for Writers of Term Papers, Theses and Dissertations*. In Chapter 9, SABR's Publications Director recommends another respected guide, the *MLA Style Manual*, and for Internet-era references he suggests *Wired Style: Principles of English Usage in the Digital Age*. It goes without saying that if your prospective publisher suggests a particular style manual, that is the one you should use.

Third, find a place to write that is free from distractions and interruptions. Writing is a solitary activity, requiring focus and concentration. If necessary, disconnect the telephone and banish the people you live with to a movie theater or to the home of a friend or relative.

Fourth, set aside sizable blocks of time, preferably two to four hours, in which to write. Few writers can compose effectively in short bursts. You'll need time to get into the flow of composing, and you'll want to keep tapping your creative energies when they emerge.

Fifth, keep small note cards and a pen or pencil handy at all times, even on the nightstand next to your bed. Since writers seldom succeed in putting their projects out of mind, ideas can and do appear suddenly and at the most inopportune times. Be prepared to record your thoughts at a moment's notice, lest they be lost.

RULE TWO: THINK BEFORE YOU WRITE

You need to prepare mentally for the task of writing. Think conceptually about what you are doing.

Know Your Audience. Ask yourself: Who will be reading my work? Readers always range from the committed expert to the casually curious, but there will be usually be a primary, target audience. Keep those readers in mind when you write. Obviously, you will write differently for *The Baseball Research Journal* or *The National Pastime* than you will for an academic journal. When writing for a general interest publication, be sure to explain terms such as "Triple Crown," because readers may not understand the reference—or they may think you have segued from baseball into horse racing. If you are writing primarily for other SABR members, you can assume a basic knowledge of baseball history and terminology. But even within SABR there may be readers who aren't familiar with your subject. These readers will not appreciate an offhand mention of HEQ, say, or The Wacks Museum. Take care not to assume too much. What is obvious to you may not be obvious to others.

Know Yourself. We've all read articles or books in which the author comes across as an uncritical advocate or as a hostile critic. Writers sometimes fall in love with their subjects and report their findings more as cheerleaders than as judicious observers. At the other extreme, familiarity can breed contempt, with the author becoming a shrill assailant rather than a fair-minded arbiter. Your should be aware of your own biases, just as you should be aware of those of others. A researcher is a truth-seeker. Although there is no such thing as a truly "objective" history—which is one reason so many histories get written—biases can be controlled. You have to make judgments about actions taken and decisions made. But try to keep emotionally at arm's length from your subject, letting the reader form conclusions from the evidence, not from your advocacy. Compare the tone and emphases of Charles C. Alexander's *Ty Cobb* and Al Stump's *Cobb* to see how very differently two authors can deal with the same subject.

Know Your Task. New information, new insights, new interpretations—these are the reasons your work will be published and read. Whether your work is biographical, historical, or statistical, your task is to present new material to readers in a way that is interesting, intelligible, and significant. In short, your task is to teach. This requires not only clarity of presentation, but an attempt to relate your findings to previous research, whenever possible, as well as to baseball history generally and perhaps even to society at large. Your writing will be easier and your readers more appreciative if you keep in mind that you are teaching about a subject, not just delivering a collection of facts and related commentary.

READY, SET, WRITE

At last you're ready to write! How do you begin?

It's a good idea to prepare a preliminary outline—especially for a book—so that you have an overall sense of the shape of the manuscript before beginning to put it together. This is the writer's equivalent of the architect's blueprint, the structural framework of the finished work. You'll probably revise the outline as you write, but, as you're doing so, you'll see how the changes fit in as part of a coherent, overall scheme. The longer your manuscript is going to be, the more complete the outline you need. A full-scale biography of James "Cool Papa" Bell would require a detailed outline. A thousand-word article on the tragic death of Ed Delahanty would probably need no formal outline at all, just a clear, chronological retelling of the incident.

Sort and organize your research materials. Depending on the length of your project, you may have several dozen or several thousand items. The organization of your outline determines how to sort the material. If you're analyzing Joe Wilhoit's 69-game hitting streak for Wichita in the Class A Western League in 1919, chronological order probably makes the most sense. A topical arrangement might be best if you're writing about Ted Williams's boyhood, since you'll be covering such aspects of his life as parents, school, friends, community, and ball playing. Proper organization of the raw materials from which you intend to create a manuscript is critical.

Note Cards. A good way to write your manuscript is to work from note cards. Because of their efficiency and flexibility, note cards are the most popular means of recording information. These cards can be either 4x6-inch or 5x8-inch ones—the familiar 3x5 cards are useful for recording bibliographic information and for taking spur-of-the-moment notes, but they're too small for serious note-taking. Notebook paper and yellow pads, on the other hand, are too large and unwieldy for convenience either in taking notes or in using those notes when writing the manuscript.

Be sure that each card contains all necessary information: (a) everything you need to document the source itself and (b) everything you think you will need from the source when you do your writing. If you use sequentially numbered 3x5 cards for your bibliography, you can then identify each source by number instead of having to record author, title, publisher, date, etc., over and over on every note card. A word of caution: Never record multiple topics on a single card. If a newspaper article contains information on, say, four topics relevant to your project, make four separate note cards. Individual cards can be slotted into their proper places in your organizational plan, whereas one card with four topics fits nowhere.

Audiovisual Materials. Audiovisual materials bring the past to life with the sights and sounds of the times. Tape-recorded oral interviews are a popular and important research tool. It's a good idea to transcribe audio tapes, or at least those parts you intend to use. The recollections of interviewees must be fact-checked, and the easiest way to do that is by means of transcriptions. To have to keep re-listening to tape cassette while you are writing is time-consuming and extremely disruptive. If an interview is short and limited in scope, you may prefer to take notes while listening to the tape.

Videotapes and films—interviews, game footage, documentaries—are increasingly popular sources. There is no alternative to making handwritten notes while viewing videos and film. Be sure to write down all identifying information, including the full title, producer, distributor, and release date. Information from videotapes and films requires documentation in much the same way that books and magazine articles do.

Photocopies. Photocopiers and microfilm reader-printers have revolutionized research. The ease of duplicating printed materials has led some researchers to use photocopies instead of notes during the writing process. That may work for a narrowly focused article, but it is seldom a good idea when writing a longer, more discursive article or a book-length manuscript. Photocopied documents are often lengthy and contain multiple topics, thus presenting organizational difficulties for the writer. For that reason, some researchers keep photocopies for reference, but take notes from the photocopies before starting to write. Others paste or tape relevant portions of photocopied text onto traditional note cards. No matter how you use photocopies, be sure that you clearly mark them with all relevant source information, preferably at the time you make the copies.

EFFECTIVE WRITING

Anyone can write, but not everyone can write brilliantly. Gifted writers, like great hitters, are rare, but most of us can become competent writers by following a few basic rules of grammar and usage.

1. *Use standard English.* In general, try to avoid jargon and slang. If such terms are necessary, define them in context if they are likely to be unknown to most readers. Most SABR members will understand *wheelhouse*, but may not know *yakker* or *green flies*. Use your judgment to decide what needs defining. The principle here is simple: You want to communicate, so use terms that readers

will understand. Along the same lines, don't use polysyllabic or obscure words needlessly. For example, use *in contrast*, not *in contradistinction*.

2. **Use complete sentences.** A sentence fragment, as you probably know, is a phrase or clause punctuated as a sentence but lacking a subject or a verb or both. Although sentence fragments can be effective when used infrequently for emphasis, they can also be annoying. Fragments are rampant in advertisements but not in most other good prose. Unless you're a skilled, fluent writer, readers are likely to view your sentence fragments as signs of questionable literacy rather than as marks of literary distinction.

3. **Use correct grammar and syntax.** Don't dangle participles. Be sure that subjects and verbs agree. A good grammar checker in a word processing program like Microsoft Word will highlight a variety of grammatical errors. Whenever you see the highlighting, check to see what the computer thinks you got wrong. (Sometimes, in my experience, the grammar checker itself will be wrong, but don't blithely assume that it is. Check out the alleged error carefully.)

4. **Use proper punctuation.** Learn how to use (and not to overuse) colons, semicolons, parentheses, and dashes. Don't put an exclamation point after every sentence you think makes a strong statement. Too many exclamation points weaken rather than strengthen your prose.

5. **Use the past tense and the active voice.** Write "Ruth homered off Tom Zachary," not "Ruth homers off Tom Zachary." Write "The Yankees won the World Series," not "The World Series was won by the Yankees."

6. **Make direct, positive statements.** "Ruth often missed curfew" is better than "Ruth did not very often make curfew." Minimize the use of inconsequential qualifiers: "He was a good hitter," not "He was a very good hitter." (If he was better than good, use *excellent* or *outstanding*.) Keep it simple. Omit needless words. Instead of "due to the fact that Ruth indulged his appetites," write "because Ruth indulged his appetites."

7. **Vary sentence structure.** This is best done by minimizing the use of "crutches" to begin sentences. I forbid my undergraduate students to start sentences in term papers with the following words—*But, However, Since, Because, Thus, Therefore, While,* and *Although*. These easy and unthinking ways of beginning sentences lead to lazy, monotonous writing. At the same time, make every

TRAVELING ESSENTIALS

by Larry Lester

1. Business cards (to show you are a certified eccentric).

2. Magnifying glass (for those hard-to-read microfilm printouts of box scores).

3. Compass (to assist you in directing lost souls and to help you navigate successfully to the library, historical society, or museum).

4. Maps (to provide directions and to estimate travel time so that you can arrive when the doors open, to maximize your visit).

5. Pencils (since some institutions do not allow pens in their archived collections).

6. Floppy disk (for downloading information from the Web, to be printed at a later date).

7. Rolls of dimes, nickels, and quarters (to pay for photocopies in case the change machine is broken; also needed for parking meters).

8. Tape recorder (depending on the nature of your research).

9. Single-lens reflex camera (if you intend to photograph pictures or documents; some institutions have copy stands with lights that you can use).

10. Extra batteries for your tape recorder and camera.

11. Highlighters (to identify special areas of attention—only on your own photo-copies, of course, not on library materials).

12. Gumdrops, Lifesavers, and/or mints (for those long hours without food; also useful for striking up library conversations).

13. A whistle, to hail cabs in downtown Manhattan and other congested metro areas.

14. Sticky notes; and

15. A friendly smile.

My motto: *We are drowning in information, but starving for knowledge.*

effort to show the relationships between and among clauses. To take a simple example, don't write *and* when you mean *but*.

8. **Avoid repeating the same words and constructions;** to wit: "He joined the Yankees in 1951. He hit .267 with 13 homers. The next year he hit .311 with 23 homers. He then hit .295 with 21 homers." Variety is the spice of writing and the way to avoid producing the literary equivalent of a monotone.

MATTERS OF STYLE

The best way to learn to write well is to read widely and analytically. When you read an article or a book that you find especially enjoyable, look at it with the eyes of a literary critic. What is it about the writing that you like? Vivid word choice? Exceptional clarity? Conversely, when you read something that is dull or confusing, ask yourself what makes it so. Too much jargon? Lack of coherence? You can learn a great deal not only from what you like to read but also from what you don't like to read.

It's important to capture the attention of the audience. Your first paragraph or two are critical in "grabbing" the reader. Just as television viewers make instantaneous decisions when surfing channels, so, too, readers decide quickly whether they want to continue reading. This doesn't mean that you need a flashy or gimmicky lead. It does mean that you must let the reader know right away what you're writing about, what special information you have to offer, and why your message is important (or at least intriguing) to your readers.

Ultimately, good writing turns on an engaging style and a clear presentation. Writing style is difficult to describe adequately. What makes a writer's style appeal to readers? Somerset Maugham, in his autobiographical *The Summing Up*, reduces stylistic criteria to just three: lucidity, simplicity, and euphony. You may agree or disagree. A clear presentation is easier to define. Once again, think of writing as teaching. Write as if you're preparing a talk for a diverse audience that knows very little about your subject. Your presentation must be well organized. It must explain your main points clearly and concisely. Starting your paragraphs with strong topic sentences will help. So will providing good transitions between paragraphs. Subheadings that set off topical divisions within the text can also assist readers in staying on track. Always and forever, keep your readers in mind.

MATTERS OF FORM: *Quotations*

Using your own words is usually the most creative and forceful way to convey ideas and information. Still, quoting directly from sources can sometimes add color and authenticity to your work. Used properly and sparingly, quotations can be enhancements. Used improperly or excessively, they can become distractions.

A quotation is an exact transcription of something written or spoken. Quotation marks signify that a person wrote or spoke exactly those words. Note the difference between writing "Joe McCarthy said 'he was not a push-button manager'" and writing "Joe McCarthy said, 'I am not a push-button manager.'" The first example is NOT a direct quote. Joe McCarthy surely didn't refer to himself as he, nor did he put his statement in the past tense. The sentence is a paraphrase of McCarthy's remark, one that pretends to be a direct quote. The second example is correct.

When to quote? There are three common situations in which quoting is likely to be preferable to using your own words.

❶ Quote when precision is important. For example: The opinion of Justice Oliver Wendell Holmes, Jr., in the Federal Baseball Club of Baltimore case in 1922; Franklin D. Roosevelt's "Green Light" letter of 1942; and Ford Frick's response to the reportedly impending Cardinals' boycott of Jackie Robinson in 1947. These are instances where including the exact language is crucial.

❷ Quote when the wording captures the essence of a person or time. Quoting Dizzy Dean's remark, "He slud into third," characterizes the great pitcher from Arkansas far better than a flat description of the play. Quoting Henry Chadwick on *chin music* and *hippodroming* conveys the language of the nineteenth-century "Father of Baseball" more graphically than any translation of the old terms.

❸ Quote when something is especially well said, as was Commissioner Bart Giamatti's admonition during the baseball strike of 1981: "O, Sovereign Owners and Princely Players, masters of amortization, tax shelters, bonuses, and deferred compensation, go back to work." Or Frenchy Bordagaray's lament after learning the amount of his fine for spitting at an umpire: It "was a little more than I expectorated."

Quoting effectively is not simply a matter of finding and inserting a good quotation here and there. It requires blending the quote with your own words to create a seamless sentence or paragraph. Most quotations are run in as words, phrases, or sentences that appear within the text itself, usually within a single paragraph. Block quotes are lengthy quotations of several sentences. They are set off from the text by being indented and printed in smaller type. Block quotes should be avoided unless you find it absolutely essential to include them. There are a couple of reasons for this. One is that readers often think block quotes are peripheral and skip over them. Another is that they remind readers of the tedious prose of too many academic theses and dissertations.

Paraphrasing

Paraphrasing is the rewording of an original statement. It is intimately related to quoting, but it isn't quoting. And it poses a danger. SABR writers sometimes jot down the content of source materials without rewording it sufficiently. By doing so, they flirt with plagiarism. Indeed, following the original wording of a source too closely is the most frequent kind of plagiarism. For plagiarism is not, it should be emphasized, limited to copying material verbatim. Near-verbatim transcription is plagiarism, too. The rule is simple: Either quote directly or use you own words almost entirely.

Footnotes and Endnotes

Your target publication may not want footnotes or endnotes. General interest publications don't require them, while most research-oriented journals insist upon one or the other. Footnotes appear at the bottom of each page. Endnotes, essentially the same thing except for location, appear all together at the end of an article or a book. The majority of SABR publications lack footnotes or endnotes, although a growing number of *BRJ* and *TNP* articles do have them. Unless the article is one of statistical analysis or is based on an obvious main source—e.g., an interview with Johnny Vander Meer—footnoting is desirable. Most readers appreciate knowing your sources of information. It allows them (a) to assess the reliability of your work and (b) to know where to look for more detail on your subject.

Articles drawn from a selected number of books and articles often include a bibliography in lieu of footnotes. This is simply a list of works consulted, showing the author, title, place of publication, publisher, and date. Preparing a bibliography is easy, if from the beginning of your research you record on 3x5 cards complete citations for each source. For more specific information about footnotes, endnotes, and bibliographies, including the proper form for each, consult one of the style manuals mentioned earlier.

POLISHING THE DRAFT

Completing a draft of the manuscript is not the end of the writing process. You must then proofread it for errors in grammar, usage, spelling, punctuation, and so on. Don't rely solely on computer grammar-check or spell-check programs. They catch only a limited number of obvious errors. A spell-check program, for example, cannot distinguish between homonyms. If you use the wrong spelling of words that sound alike—*there* instead of *their* or *they're*, for instance, the computer won't know it and can't tell you.

After proofreading, go back over the manuscript and revise it with an eye to improving style and presentation. Ask yourself: Is my meaning clear? Is this the best way to express it? After revising the draft, set it aside for a few days or even a week. Then read it again with fresh eyes and rewrite as necessary. You may be surprised to find how much you can improve even your already revised draft.

Finally, read the manuscript aloud to yourself. When reading silently, your mind automatically corrects errors and omissions because it knows what you intended to write. Reading aloud requires greater concentration and attention to how the piece actually "reads." The most effective way to do this—and to proofread at the same time—is to read your text aloud to someone who is following along with another copy. He or she will spot errors that you might overlook when reading the manuscript by yourself.

SUBMITTING THE MANUSCRIPT

You are now ready to submit a final copy of the manuscript to a publisher. Make sure you send it in the form the publisher requires. Use 10- or 12-point type (pica or elite, respectively, on a typewriter) or 10-, 11-, or 12-point type on a word processor. Double-space everything—text, block quotes, footnotes, bibliography, and all else. Leave one-inch margins around the page—top, bottom, and both sides. Number pages consecutively, preferably in the upper right-hand corner. Follow any specific requirements or preferences indicated on the publisher's style sheet.

Make the final copy as neat and accurate as possible. Avoid submitting a manscript containing strikeovers, handwritten corrections, or typographical errors. Ultimately, publishing decisions are based on the quality and importance of the material. But initial appearances are important. A sloppy appearance suggests carelessness in other areas, including research. And the fewer the editorial changes required, the less likelihood of errors in the final book or article.

Submit your manuscript in both hard copy (on paper) and, if you used a computer, on a standard disk. The label on the disk should contain your name, the title of the work, and the word-processing software program you used. Never submit your manuscript to more than one publisher at a time. That is a serious breach of etiquette, especially when submitting an article to a journal or an annual.

Expect prompt acknowledgment of the receipt of your manuscript, but not an immediate decision regarding publication. The publisher's decision may take several weeks. Some periodicals, like *BJR* and *TNP*, have a single editor responsible for all aspects of publication. Delays may occur because of a busy schedule or because the manuscript has been sent to one or more reviewers. Be patient.

THE FINAL STAGES

Upon accepting your manuscript, all book publishers and most periodicals will ask you to sign a publishing agreement. Whether a formal printed contract or a letter of agreement, this is a legal document that stipulates the rights and obligations of the publisher and the author. The basic terms of publishing agreements are fairly standard throughout the industry, so unless changes have been made in the one you receive (with a request that you initial the changes), you need not be concerned. Do read the agreement carefully, though. Ordinarily, you will retain the copyright to your work, but the publisher assumes control over most aspects of printing, design, advertising, and promotion. Don't expect to be able to decide on the layout, font, print size, placement of illustrations, or, in the case of a book, the jacket design or even the title of the book.

At least one editor will go over your manuscript word by word, line by line. Ernest Hemingway and Maya Angelou received editing, and so will you. Authors sometimes find it hard to relinquish something they have worked on so long and so hard. Accepting editorial revisions can be even more difficult. That is understandable. But think twice before complaining because some of your words have been changed or because certain sentences are deleted or rewritten. The editor is reviewing your work as an objective observer. His or her role is to improve your writing and adhere to the publication's stylistic preferences. If you feel the editor has distorted your meaning or done unnecessary violence to your prose, speak up. Otherwise, be grateful for the assistance. The edited manuscript may be returned to you for your approval, or it may go straight into page proof.

In days past, you would have received a set of galley proofs—long typeset sheets without pagination. Today, because of computer technology, you are more likely to receive a set of page proofs—typeset pages that look as if they're ready to be bound and shipped. Don't be deceived. That same computer technology makes it easier than it used to be with galleys to correct misspellings, improper punctuation, or any other minor errors. You can't rewrite at this stage, though. Nor should you have to, if you've been conscientious about your writing up to this point. Resist the urge to rewrite. If you think a major change is absolutely necessary, clear it with the editor right away.

An index, if one is being done, is prepared at the page-proof stage. Journal articles are limited in scope and thus need no index. Books, however, usually do. If your publisher will include an index—and you should make a strong case for it—you must decide whether to prepare it yourself or pay for a professional indexer. A professional is usually hired by the publisher and paid for out of your future royalties. Doing an index yourself is certainly cheaper, but unless you know the basics of index preparation, you will probably get a better index by paying for it. You, the author, know your book's contents better than anyone else. A professional indexer may know nothing whatever about your subject, but he or she is objective, experienced, and able to see the book from the perspective of the reader.

The purpose of an index is to allow a reader to locate every pertinent concept, person, place, or event mentioned in the book. A book on baseball in New York City in the 1950s, for example, would include index entries for Mickey Mantle, the Brooklyn Dodgers, the Polo Grounds, continental expansion, racial integration, umpires, and the World Series. An index shouldn't include everything possible, only those items a reader might reasonably be expected to look for. If, for instance, in a biography of Babe Ruth, you mention that the Bambino drank chrysanthemum tea during his 1934 trip to Japan, there is no need to index chrysanthemum tea, as readers are not likely to look for that.

Indexing adds immeasurably to a nonfiction book's utility. Librarians, realizing this, tend to favor books with indexes over those with none. If you're doing an index yourself, the most efficient method is to go through the page proofs and record entries on separate 3x5 cards every time they appear. If Ty Cobb is mentioned on pages 59, 60, and 61, write "Cobb, Ty, 59," "Cobb, Ty, 60," and "Cobb, Ty, 61" on three separate cards. If the page contains more than just a mere mention, jot down a brief descriptive note: "Cobb, Ty, attitudes toward blacks, 142." Toss the cards into a pile. When you have completed all of the cards, alphabetize them.

When you create the final index, if any of your entries—say, Ty Cobb—appears on fewer than five or six cards, simply record the page numbers: "Cobb, Ty, 7, 19, 32, 44, 109." If an entry appears on more than six cards, however, divide the cards into one or more topic subentries to rid the reader of the burden of checking every page—"Cobb, Ty, 7, 19, 32, 44, 109; childhood, 14-17; batting titles, 88-89, 102-03, 107, 114-15; racial attitudes, 76-79, 142; managerial career, 183-88.

Once you've sent off the corrected page proofs and the index (if you're done the index yourself), there's nothing to do but wait for publication. Being published is a thrill. The first sight of your work in print brings a rush of pride in accomplishment as well as satisfaction in knowing that your research will be available to readers, now and in the future. It is also a humbling experience. You will appreciate your debt to other researchers, and you will recognize the effort that goes into transforming research notes into a manuscript worthy of publication.

The journey from the birth of an idea to the full maturity of a published article or book isn't always easy, but it's a journey you'll be glad you took.

ABOUT THE CHAPTER AUTHORS

Gerald Tomlinson, a writer, editor, and publisher, wrote *The Baseball Research Handbook* for SABR in 1987, with the able assistance of two dozen SABR contributors. His baseball articles have appeared in *The National Pastime*, *The Baseball Research Journal*, *Minor League History Journal*, *The SABR Review of Books*, *The Cooperstown Review*, and *Spitball*. With A. D. Suehsdorf and the late Ralph Horton he was a member of the SABR Publications Committee in 1990-91. Much of his non-baseball writing has been in the fields of mystery fiction and true crime.

Steve Gietschier has been Director of Historical Records at *The Sporting News* since 1986 and a SABR member since 1987. A professional archivist since 1975, he has spoken and written widely about baseball history and archival research, and he has assisted many other SABR members in pursuing their research projects. He served two years on the SABR Board of Directors and chairs the *TSN*-SABR Baseball Research Award Committee.

Andy McCue, a writer and editor, is chair of SABR's Bibliography Committee. He is the author of *Baseball by the Books*, a bibliography of baseball fiction that won the 1991 SABR-Macmillan Award for baseball research. His baseball articles have appeared in *The Sporting News*, *Nine*, *Grandstand Baseball Annual*, *The National Pastime*, *The SABR Review of Books*, and *Baseball's First Stars*. In his other life, he is a business and economics columnist for *The Press-Enterprise* in Riverside, California.

Jed Hathaway is a librarian with the Minneapolis Public Library and has been heavily involved with that library's Internet reference services. He is the originator and principal project director of SABR's "Baseball Index," an online index to the entirety of baseball literature. A SABR member since 1988, he has been active in promoting and facilitating the Society's use of the Internet. He is the author of *The Senior Professional Baseball Association* (1992) and the bibliography for *The Senior League Encyclopedia* (1998).

Neal Traven was born while the Whiz Kids were closing in on the National League pennant. He will forever be scarred because in 1980 he left the country on vacation the day before the Phillies clinched the NL East, returning the day after they won the World Series. A SABR member since 1984, he co-chairs the Statistical Analysis Committee. He currently resides in Portsmouth, New Hampshire. In his spare time he is an epidemiologist working with administrative claims and medical records from half a million Medicare beneficiaries in Maine, Vermont, and New Hampshire.

Cappy Gagnon is the Coordinator of Stadium Personnel for the University of Notre Dame. His baseball writings have appeared in *The Baseball Research Journal*, *The National Pastime*, *Nineteenth Century Stars*, *The Ballplayers*, *The Baseball Chronology*, *Total Baseball*, and *Grandstand Baseball Annual*. He is working on a book, *Anson to Yaz*, about the seventy Notre Dame men who have played in the major leagues. A SABR member since 1977, he served on the Board of Directors for seven years, including two terms as President. He founded both the Los Angeles (Allan Roth) and South Bend (Lou Criger) Chapters of SABR. He serves as the chair of the Collegiate Committee.

Mark Rucker searches the world for baseball imagery, both obscure and revelatory. He has co-authored biographical books on Babe Ruth and Ted Williams, worked on historical tomes covering baseball in the nineteenth and twentieth centuries, and provided picture research on numerous films, including Ken Burns' *Baseball*. He has also provided imagery for ballpark installations, book and magazine covers, baseball products, and packaging. His latest work is the first pictorial history of the sport in Cuba, *Smoke: The Romance and Lore of Cuban Baseball*.

Tom Shieber, Webmaster at the National Baseball Hall of Fame and Museum, has been a SABR member since 1980. An avid baseball picture researcher for over twenty years, Tom founded SABR's Pictorial History Committee in 1995 and has chaired the committee since that time. He has served on the SABR Board of Directors since 1997.

Mark Alvarez has been SABR's Publications Director and the editor of most of its publications since 1992. A former magazine editor, he is the author of four books, the co-author of two, and has written dozens of articles on topics ranging from baseball to architecture to travel and the out-of-doors. He has recently laid down his hometown duties as selectman and winder of the town clock.

Larry Gerlach is Professor of History at the University of Utah. He has published numerous books and articles on colonial and revolutionary America, the Ku Klux Klan, lynching, and sports. His baseball publications include *The Men in Blue: Conversations* *with Umpires*, and articles in *The Journal of Sport History*, *Baseball's First Stars*, *The Baseball Research Journal*, *The National Pastime*, *The SABR Review of Books*, and *The Cooperstown Review*. A founding member of the Umpires and Rules Committee, he has also served on the SABR Board of Directors, 1991-97, and as President, 1997-99.

INDEX